It's OK to Leave the Plantation
The New Underground Railroad

John O Berkeley
Stay Right

Written by
Clarence Mason Weaver

Edited by
Julie Reeder

Reeder Publishing

It's OK to Leave the Plantation
The New Underground Railroad

Published by Reeder Publishing. Written permission must be
secured from the publisher or author to use or reproduce any
part of this book, including electronic or mechanical copying,
photocopying, recording, or by any information storage and
retrieval system except for brief quotations in critical reviews or
articles. For information address: Reeder Publishing, 1114 S.
Main St., Fallbrook, CA 92028, or Email: vnews1@tfb.com.
For information concerning speaking engagements or reprinting,
contact Clarence Mason Weaver at P.O. Box 1764,
Oceanside, California, 92051. Phone or fax (760) 758-7448.
Email address is masonweaver@masonweaver.com
To order additional copies of this book, call 1-760-758-7448.

Printed in the United States of America

First Edition printed July, 1996
Second Edition printed May, 1998
Third Edition, fourth printing July, 2000
ISBN No. 0-9655218-1-8

Reeder Publishing

Dedication

This book is dedicated to my Lord and Savior Jesus Christ who calls all of us from slavery to freedom!

Also to my mother Marcella Weaver, whose wisdom led her to choose a Godly man as my father. To my father, Reverend Waverly Weaver Jr., for his example of how a man worships God, loves his community and protects his family.

And a special thanks to my wife Brynda, the world's most beautiful woman, for making me the world's most blessed man. And to my sons, Michael and Brian, to whom the future belongs.

For my wife Brynda, the world's most beautiful woman

Thanks and Acknowledgments

As I began this second edition of the book I found myself in a curious situation. The 1998 elections were beginning and many of my friends and associates were busy with campaigning. The professional skills and expertise I utilized on the first manuscript were in great demand. I recognize the tremendous time restraints and personal dedication of so many of my friends and wanted to publicly thank them. I can only list a few, so please forgive me if I omit you.

Sharon Newman, for editing the second draft.

Julie Reeder of Reeder Publishing, and editor of the Fallbrook/ Bonsall Village News, for publishing and updating the project.

Carl Polizzi for his talent in the cover design.

I know I have not mentioned many, but I am grateful to all.

Contents

Chapter Four

Chapter Five

Chapter Six

"Victory comes

to the faithful,

not to the strong;

stay faithful."

Mason Weaver

True wisdom comes by learning from life and not repeating mistakes

Wisdom does not come from surviving but from thriving. This book discusses some of the family and environmental contributions that led to my change from liberal to conservative. It also discusses how Black Americans came from slavery to freedom.

How did black people end up in America as slaves? How did Africa, a powerful continent, with a rich history and highly structured societies, end up colonized like children by the Europeans? This book outlines the spiritual and social reasons Africa submitted to the Europeans.

The Africans were never really slaves in America. If we were slaves, there would have been no reason for whips and chains. You are only a slave if you think like a slave. The Africans were captives in America and resisted as much as possible. The captors had to develop self-hatred, worthlessness, and hopelessness in the Africans to make them think they were slaves. ___It's OK To Leave The Plantation___ examines the "Plantation mentality" that still plagues us today. The Plantation Mentality is a system that discourages independence and character and encourages reliance on masters or appointed tribal chiefs in our community.

Instead of complaining about how the white man has us down, we need to stop whining and start progressing. We have accomplished a great deal in America since slavery and we should highlight this. Instead of whining, let us give our children hope by pointing out the endless possibilities.

The purpose of the civil rights movement was to remove legal barriers and allow Black Americans to compete. It was not an attempt to make white America like us or appreciate us. We have won the legal battles; now it is time we step out and take advantage of those rights. We owe it to the honor of those who suffered in the struggle, those unsung heroes who hoped for this day. We now have the responsibility to take advantage of what they died for: to be successful right here in America.

The plantation mentality has only one purpose: to create more anger and resentment among Black Americans and more guilt among White Americans

The only solution our black leaders have is demanding more from the "slave masters." All we hear is what they owe us, not what we can earn. They want us to be repaid for all the labor given free to America. They want reparations, but this would put the master in a position to grant what is not his to give; it is already ours for the taking.

If we grant some kind of reparations to Black American descendants of slaves, every American with a drop of black blood would claim the benefits. This is a program that could never work logistically, nor is it warranted socially. If we get reparations, will we have to repay all of the programs we have received? ***It's OK To Leave The Plantation*** examines the reasons reparations will not work.

Not since reconstruction have black people been so successful. The decade of the 1980's saw more prosperity and individual freedoms than ever before. We should find out what happened during the 1980's and demand that we do it again. This book documents the economic achievements of Black Americans during the "Reagan Years."

Doctor King's dream was not only that of a color-blind society, but a victimless society. King wanted equal rights—not special rights. The current media-appointed black leaders need victims to lead and un-motivated masses in order to gain power. The real dream of Dr. King was of a place where we all were leaders and did not need to follow anyone. The principles of Dr. King have been stolen by renegade black social pimps who only create violence for their benefit. This book traces the beginnings of the modern "tribal chiefs" and how their power is distributed.

When the nation has true power on the family level, it is truly a free and powerful nation. We will examine the Affirmative Action debate. We will trace the beginning of the end of the stranglehold by the current civil rights leaders. Black Americans are beginning to think and vote like individuals.

What were the goals of the civil rights movements of the 1950's and 1960's? Equal rights or special rights, independence or codependence? We will look at some of the pathology of our civil rights leaders as they struggle with the aftermath of a movement that has been won. We will also discuss what to do with the victory!

We need to be educated, motivated, and stimulated! The black community has been pinned up too long, and we are ready to burst into mainstream America with full force. We have been the ones harmed by liberal good intentions. We have been the ones whose families have been devastated by the failed social welfare programs. We have been the main beneficiaries of the public schools' mis-education. However, we are ready to move out of it. We only need the spark. Black Americans have begun to recognize their conservative roots and heritage and will begin to act upon them. All we need is for someone to stand up and say *"It's OK To Leave The Plantation."*

This book examines some other celebrations, superstitions and contrived traditions being substituted for the strong culture and honor we have had as a people. The danger of recognizing false traditions and holidays is the loss of the lessons of our real history. Culture and traditions of a people are made of their history, not fantasy. The celebration of Kwanzaa as a traditional African holiday is not only untrue, but, in fact, weakens the real rich heritage our ancestors gave us.

Now that the civil rights movement is over and we can compete in the political arena, why don't we? Real political power comes from organizing along lines of principle, not those of race or culture. Real issues affect all people; therefore, there are no racial, sexual, age, or cultural issues.

We can see the dismantling of the tribalistic control over the black community and explore the new avenue open to us: freedom. This will take independent thought and it is our final lesson. For hundreds of years others have thought for us—the master, overseer, preacher, civil rights leader and one political party. However, freedom is an individual journey, not a group journey. Let us explore the individual journey to independence.

Clarence Mason Weaver
Oceanside, California   July, 1996

Chapter One

My Journey from Liberalism to Conservatism

"Victory comes to the faithful, not to the strong; stay faithful."
                                                    Mason Weaver

My journey from a Berkeley liberal to a conservative has not been a difficult one. I have not changed; America has changed. I would still be a militant revolutionary today if there were still "colored only" signs allowed. If police could still openly abuse us with no recourse, I would still be marching. Had the poll tax and grandfather clauses still existed, you would find me still protesting.

This journey came about as America turned towards her conscience and began to realize her principles. There is still racism and discrimination, but that is not the point. The point is that there are no longer "legal" barriers. The civil rights movement was a struggle to remove the "legal" barriers and allow equal opportunity to all. What it has turned into is equal opportunity for all to be under the master. Now, Black and White people are on the plantation together, depending on government as the master.

It seems like all we have managed to achieve are better programs from the master. The struggle was not for better government programs; it was not about a better plantation system. It was about getting off the plantation. Instead of freedom, more of us are enslaved. We have more government control over our lives than ever before. However, there is one thing different about this plantation system: it depends on volunteers. We now have the right to participate in the American dream.

By 1968, I was tired of a system that called me names and expected me to accept it. I was tired of a country that would allow me to fight in her wars but not allow me full access to her economic system. I was tired of a nation full of hate, guilt and greed and no love for itself. The America of 1968 was a tired place to be and one that needed to be changed.

I entered the military because racist teachers would not allow me to enter college. I endured openly racist military officers and enlisted men, and still obtained promotions. Finally, I began to associate myself with other frustrated and angry Black men. We compounded our anger and began to look at ourselves as victims of a slave master instead of military men. The old saying "misery loves company" is true, and we continued to look for reasons to be unhappy with our condition. We began to protest our condition and treatment, then demanded recognition and respect. We began to change things on board our ship in a small but very important way.

The ship's library began carrying Black authors. The bookstore began carrying Black products and even the captain recognized that the "Afro" hairstyle was important enough to change our haircut regulations. I was beginning to think that talking to "the man" would make him aware of the harm he was doing, and that would cause change. We were beginning high school completion courses and even college credit courses on the ship. We were improving community relations by working with children as their mentors. I thought it was really working out. I continued to think that way, until someone dropped 2800 pounds of metal plates on me. The official Naval investigation recorded the weight of the "accident" as 1700 pounds of steel and iron.

The official investigation did not happen until I insisted

from my hospital bed. It occurred weeks after the event and missed some things, including approximately 1000 pounds of aluminum, black iron and even chicken wire that fell. Only I and one other person on that ship realized what had really happened, and we both knew it was no accident!

I ended up disabled and separated from the Navy, living with my uncle in Richmond, California. Although I was in constant pain, I enrolled into Merritt College in Oakland, California. I had back and hip injuries that kept me from prolonged periods of sitting, walking or standing. I was angry, and I blamed the racist conditions on that ship for cheating me out of four years of training. I could no longer work as a welder, shipfitter or pipefitter because of my permanent disabilities, but I was not going to be a bum.

All of us can remember important historical dates in our lives. The day of JFK's assassination, Pearl Harbor, and man landing on the moon will stick in the minds of all who lived through those experiences.

Personal dates like marriage, the birth of a child, or the death of a loved one will also forge permanent memories for us. I have one such memory which I reflect on every anniversary. I may not think about it during the preceding week, but on August 11, I always find myself sitting and thinking about that morning back in 1971.

I was a 21-year-old sailor away from home, free of parental control, strong and enjoying my career in the Navy. I had a hard job as a shipfitter, pipefitter and welder. I lived off base and enjoyed a full social life with many friends. That year I purchased my first car, rented my first apartment and was beginning to find my place in society.

My job was demanding: welding heavy metal plates and fabricating steam piping for other ships. This work kept me in top physical condition. I was learning a marketable skill and looking forward to a rewarding job at one of the busy shipyards when my discharge came the following year.

However, my discharge was not to come that year. I was never to work as a shipfitter or pipefitter again. After August 11, 1971, I would never pick up a welding torch, bend pipe or ever cut steel again. On that date, at 9:05 in the morning, someone tried to kill me and nearly succeeded. That someone was a known racist who preached race-hatred on board the ship. He targeted me out of anger for my political activities on the ship. He was in a position to drop those metal plates on me because of my willingness to work with someone who considered me their enemy. I did not know he was my enemy--just that he was my competitor. It was almost a fatal error.

I never had a problem working with competitors; they made you stronger. I had served in Vietnam and understood the difference between a competitor and an enemy. An enemy was to be destroyed without mercy. You could not work with him, compromise with him nor tolerate him. The enemy was to be challenged. I had also played sports and understood genuine competition. No matter how strong the competition was, you could play by the rules and even learn from them. You never wanted to hurt the competitors and never considered them evil. To me this shipmate and I were competitors, not enemies. I did not think he hated me.

That Wednesday morning I looked into his eyes as he released 2800 pounds of steel, black iron and aluminum plates to fall on me. As I turned to run, they caught me on my left hip and pinned me against the wall on my right side. The force hit me with such power that it crushed my fiberglass/steel helmet against the wall. With broken ribs, ruptured spleen, crushed pelvis, and hip and back injuries, I found myself screaming in pain. My eyes were shut, closed in agony, as the total weight settled on me. When I opened my eyes, I was staring at him. Only he and I knew what had really happened. The look in his eyes was one of unemotional contempt. It was the expression of someone who had finally gotten rid of an annoying fly or rat. That expression fueled my racial hatred and anger for years. That expression caused me to give up on compromising. I was then determined that no one would ever be in such a position over me again. I understood that to some people (even shipmates), I was considered an enemy.

I would spend the next few weeks at Balboa Naval Hospital in San Diego. My career was over, and I lay in that bed broken and in pain. It is strange how your priorities can change so quickly. That fateful morning I had been wondering if I would get a home run on the softball team that following week. One hour after work began, I was longing just to take a deep breath on my own.

One moment I was a strong, young, self-reliant man, and the next moment I was dependent on strangers to wet my dried tongue and feed me soup through a straw. I could fill this book on the things we take for granted. I could speak only in a whisper because the vibrations of my voice would hurt my back. The nervous tapping of visitors at the foot of my bed was like a sledgehammer up my spine. I never knew how everything focused on your back.

Nevertheless, I had to set goals--or face a lifetime of lying in that bed. I used to stare down to the end of my ward where I found my two new goals in life. At the end of the ward were a door and a water fountain. The door led to the men's room, and the patients used the water fountain. My goal in life became very simple! One day I would walk to that fountain, take a drink, and enter that door, on my own.

It may seem strange having such goals, but you must start somewhere. Depending on others to feed you, clean you and even exercise you will create the most simplistic goals. I eventually took that walk and it was the coolest, smoothest drink of water I have ever had. I eventually gained control over my mind and body and walked out of that hospital. However, I would never be the same man.

Gone was that boy from the foothills of the Ozark Mountains, gone was my childish innocence. Gone was the nonchalant wait for the future--my future had come crashing down on me in more ways than one.

From that day forward for the rest of my life, I will suffer some kind of pain. The Navy eventually classified my injuries as permanent and discharged me. I had to retrain myself by enrolling in college, and doing so either on medication or in pain. I admit to having much anger against the person responsible. I knew it was racial and I allowed that to cause me to become a racist person.

My hatred was irrational and could be kept alive only by irrational thinking. That person did not represent the White race--how could I then hate the entire White race? White shipmates rescued me that day. White people gave me first aid and took care of me in the hospital.

Even in my radicalism at Berkeley, I knew hating was counter-productive for my future. It was eating me up and preventing me from learning and developing. However, the pain would not go away. Every day it was there reminding me of that day in 1971. Some days I used a cane, other days medication, but always the pain and restriction on my life were there.

However, as the years have gone by, I have found something greater than racial hatred. It is called forgiveness. I had reason to hate; therefore, I also had the power to forgive. I could have accepted this attack upon my life as a reason to attack back at White America. I could have allowed that person to direct my entire life. However, once I tried forgiveness, the weight of hatred was lifted off me.

I found it weighed much more than 2800 pounds. The Biblical principle of forgiveness works and was freedom for me. It took a spiritual heart transplant to give me a forgiving heart.

I am writing about this spiritual, Biblical, Christian change because I am hearing the demands for an apology for slavery. White people and Black people are debating whether descendants of slave owners should apologize to the descendants of slaves. As a person once tied up with those emotions, I have a suggestion. Instead of waiting for the apology, try forgiving. Instead of demanding that the master's descendants recognize the harm, try releasing the legacy, in forgiveness.

If we became a forgiving nation instead of an apologetic one, we would also become a victimless one. Once I understood how much I had been forgiven, it was also clear how little in comparison I could forgive others.

Many people may want to know what happened to the sailor who dropped 2800 pounds of metal on me. Others could be interested in the official investigation of the incident.

I do not consider it very important. The story is not so much about my accident but about forgiveness and the freedom such action will give you. I am offering some alternative solutions to the current debate over an apology for slavery. If someone thinks they have been harmed by society, that person has more power to forgive than to insist on an apology. I have no control over someone else's apology, but I can control my own forgiveness.

I used the story of a racist shipmate's attempt to kill me to illustrate the years of hatred I endured along with the constant pain of my injuries. I went through college as a radical student at U.C. Berkeley and blamed White America in general--and that racist shipmate in particular--for the lost opportunities of a healthy life.

The Navy has classified me as permanently disabled and the pains of those injuries will be with me for the rest of my life. I have no control over that, but I do have control over my reaction to it.

No disciplinary action was taken against him, but everyone on that ship knew that any incident involving this man and me would never have been by accident. We both had reputations of being militant and antagonistic toward each other. At the time, I was a Black racist, he was a White racist, and we spent many days debating the racial issues that existed in 1971. I considered myself a supporter of the Black Panthers, and he seemed to think the White race was superior. It still did not dawn on me that he was a danger to me. I did not have any personal feelings toward him one way or the other. I felt he was wrong politically and thought we had inspiring debates over our differences.

Looking back, the officers should have never allowed us to work that closely together. Something was guaranteed to happen. After my accident and with the suspicion of the crew, racial tension tore the ship apart. Many of my militant friends were bent on revenge, and the normally dangerous job of a shipfitter became unbearable.

That ship was a microcosm of America in the 1970's and the America of the 1990's. It was truly a "multi-cultural" ship with diverse beliefs and understanding. It was not a "Navy" culture; it was Black, White, Northern and Southern culture. We were never united. We disliked each other because of our differences. I do not want to live in a country like that.

That man did not want to kill me; hatred influenced him to act. I can look back through the pain and anger and clearly see he was remorseful. I believe he wanted to say he was sorry, but his pride and mine did not allow it. When my shipmates visited me in the hospital, he was with them. I knew he was uncomfortable and could not make eye contact with me. As I have said, only he and I knew. Looking back, his harshness was gone. His militant stance was much softer. He had tried to kill someone out of hatred and it had an effect on him. From my hospital bed, I asked him the question, "What happened?" However, we both already knew the answer.

There must have been twenty other sailors around that room visiting me. With the racial tension of the ship as high as it was, they all fell quiet for his answer. "What happened," I repeated my question to the hushed room. "I don't know, I don't know!" The answer came in a whisper almost inaudible. Gone were the boldness, the pride, and the superior attitude. Looking back, I believed he recognized that he had tried to kill a competitor, not his enemy.

I have never spoken another word to him since then, and I have no idea what has become of him. However, I hope he has found release from his pain as I have from mine. I hope that he has discovered the power of forgiveness. As he has grown into maturity, I pray he has grown to forgive himself. It would be a terrible sentence for him to go through life believing I still hated him. If we can forgive our former enemies of war and work with them, why not forgive the men we served with in war?

If my grandfather can work with the Germans he fought against in Europe, if my father can live with the Koreans, and if I am to see my country trade with Vietnam, what is a little disagreement between shipmates? How long do we keep the pain? How long do we fight the war? How long do we hold on to the hate? I have never had the chance to tell him, but... Allen, if you are out there, my friend, I have forgiven you.

Once I forgave him for the pain and agony he had caused me, I began to look at the anger I had for others. I still hated White people for their ancestors' actions. Clearly, I needed to work on forgiving more than just an old shipmate.

However, that forgiveness had to come after my discovery of who I was as a man, as an American and as a Christian. I was in an environment that did not encourage forgiveness, only victimhood. Our emotions were being used by people who had other goals in mind.

Communists, feminists, revolutionaries, anti-capitalists and every other group that needed a weak and divided America joined into the call for civil rights. They marched with us, met with us and pretended to understand us, but they did not want what we wanted. We wanted freedom; they wanted to become the new masters. Because the nation and the community were so easily led by their emotions, rational thought was shut out of the debate. There was a lot of money and power in managing the down-and-out. It was usually given to people and organizations that would never have gained such power without the problems.

Soon other groups began to organize for funding and benefits. If you were a victim, you got special treatment without the hard work. If you belonged to a victim class, jobs, contracts, education and housing were opened to you. You did not have to be Black; you could be female, handicapped, poor, a gang member, an immigrant, drug-addicted or under-educated. However, what you could not have been was self-reliant, ambitious and certainly not a member of the rich, male, White elitist group.

The San Francisco/Oakland Bay area of the late 1960's and early 1970's was the worldwide center of this victim movement. I was sucked into the system out of its pure power, but it did not fool most of us.

I began to understand "poverty managers." My Democratic friends understood one thing. If you put poor people in one location, you are guaranteed to accomplish certain things. Despite the rhetoric, you are guaranteed to breed poverty, drugs, gangs, teen pregnancies and high unemployment. You are also guaranteed to breed "Democratic voters." I looked and could never find a "poor neighborhood" voting Republican. The liberal Democratic friends of mine understood: the poorer the community the stronger its vote for them. Did the Democrats really want poverty? They had the statistics--the more money the people had control over, the less need they would have for the liberal leadership.

As my senior year came, I began to lose confidence in the liberals' good intentions. I wanted to look at the results of their policies, not their promises. Once I looked, instead of following the emotional ranting, the rest was easy.

Because of my Black History training, I understood the plantation system. I understood the mechanism put in place to keep the slaves dependent upon master for every daily need. Because I understood it as a system of control, not a system of racism, I was able to recognize it when it was used against White America.

I saw all of us Americans being tricked back onto the plantation of dependency. I watched as they attacked our schools by not teaching, only indoctrinating. No Constitutional training on government doctrines such as the Constitution or Federalist papers was taught. I watched them encourage sexual activities for the young, ensuring poverty and thus dependency upon the government masters. I watched as our leaders surrendered American sovereignty to overseas competitors by limiting the competitive edge of American entrepreneurship, research and development. I watched so much government regulation, control and restrictions that no one had any real freedoms left. We were all becoming slaves, and I fought against slavery.

Why have we been building the old plantation system again? Why have we been accepting the master's system? I recognized the system and it was colorblind. It did not care about your race, sex, or culture--only your fears and

11

dependencies. We all were acting like sheep and the master was the sheepherder. I waited for the leaders to lead; I waited for the announcement that we were not going to allow America to be surrendered. I waited in vain for those demanding to participate in America to recognize she was being destroyed. I was not fighting for a return of the old system.

Merritt College in Oakland was considered the founding location of the Black Panther Party. Huey Newton, Bobby Seale, Eldridge Cleaver and others supposedly started the party while attending that college. The reputation of the Party was strong, and its influence was felt even by the type of instructors on campus.

My history requirements were met by studying the history of Africans who were kidnapped and brought to America as slaves. My foreign language requirement was Swahili, and I joined the new age of Black awareness and culture. I wore my dashiki, Afro hairstyle, dark sunglasses and an attitude. Although I hung out at the unofficial Black Panther headquarters at Jimmy's Lamppost in Oakland, something was different. I still did not feel the total anger with America that everyone else did. I thought it was because I was older than most of the other students and had been to Vietnam. That was only part of it, though. The rest was a total distaste of blaming others for our condition instead of concentrating on solutions.

All I heard from the liberal professors, civic leaders, politicians and preachers was failure and hopelessness. At Merritt College and Berkeley I took many Black History courses and lectures and felt I had a complete understanding of my culture. When I applied for my degree from Merritt College in 1974, they asked me when I would be applying for my second degree. I had taken so many Black history courses I qualified for a degree in that discipline as well.

I heard the professors state that Democrats were the party for the poor and Republicans were the party for the rich. Which one would I want to be? Eventually it dawned on me. If Democrats really thought their power and votes came from poor people, would they not want as many poor as possible? If Democrats thought Republicans gained power when people became rich or had the hope of becoming rich, would they not want to stop this? I saw all of the "get the rich" laws and restrictions and wondered if they were not simply placing barriers on Black people becoming rich.

I began fighting for equal rights, not special rights. I demanded to be independent, not codependent. I resented the call of the tribal chiefs that I must follow them; I pre-

"Bwana Mason," freshman in college-1972

ferred to follow God. Since God follows no man's race or culture, why should I? But with all of the disillusion, with all of the hopelessness, my education gave me one thing: confidence. Once I knew all of the things we had done as a people, all of the things we had struggled through, I knew nothing could stop us except ourselves.

I was working for California Democrat Congressmen Pete Stark and George Miller and felt their liberal policies were rooted in great intentions and even some personal sacrifices. Nevertheless, I was waiting for someone to recognize the results—they were killing us. Welfare was worse, crime was increasing, education was beginning to fail, and everyone wanted more of the same. I was waiting for someone to say not only that what we were doing was failing, but also it seemed that some were prof-

Mason with Congressman George Miller

14

iting from it. Nevertheless, no one was saying it, and no one was speaking the truth. I lost all confidence in the political and social leaders of the 1960's and 1970's. I felt they were all social pimps keeping the people on the plantation.

Finally, I graduated from the University of California at Berkeley in 1975. It was the hardest thing I had done. In three years (from the winter of 1972 through the summer of 1975) I had overcome severe pain and physical disabilities and obtained three college degrees. I had studied all night, taking a full load and more, plus summer school and financial burdens, and I had conquered it. My self-esteem was at an all-time high. I was the first of my parents' children to enter college or the military. They were focusing on my life as an example to shoot for and

U.C. Berkeley Graduation 1975

15

we all benefited and celebrated. But as soon as I went out looking for a job, I found condescending White employers and applicants asking if I received my college degree from Berkeley "by Affirmative Action." They assumed my degrees were not received by hard work, intelligence, or self-determination but by some benevolent White program allowing me to compete with them.

I then obtained a job with the Department of Energy and became a Senior Contract Specialist. There I had a Confidential Security Clearance and was negotiating multi-million dollar government contracts, still facing White and Black people assuming my education and job came by the graces of Affirmative Action. I began to realize what I only had a hint of in college: we had been tricked back onto the plantation. The victories of the civil rights movement had been stolen by smiling faces and promises of help by government programs. Every problem in the Black community became a problem only a government program could fix. We were no longer picking cotton but allowing our votes to be picked by one party. We found ourselves on an inner-city plantation run by Black overseers (Black leaders) who went to the master (government) for us. We found ourselves dependent on Master for jobs, education, medical benefits, and even permission to like ourselves. Black Americans had begun to prey on each other out of frustration and despair. Our plight was worse than the original plantation in many ways.

At least then we married the mother of our children, and our wives did not have to fear the men. At least during slavery, the community considered education an issue worth losing their life over. Today, not only are we not willing to die for good education, we will not even go down to the school. I watched the things I had fought for come into existence only to see the people going back to the plantation. It reminded me of the children of Israel complaining about the harshness of the desert.

Some wanted to go back to Egypt and not on to the Promised Land. Well, I was going to the Promised Land and no tribal chief or White slaveholder was going to stop me. I had seen too much and had gone through too many sacrifices to give up on my people and myself. No one was sounding the alarm; no one was giving the information. I felt like the lone child standing on the street watching the parade and saying: "the Emperor has no clothes."

Everyone knows this system does not work for us; everyone knows it works only for the plantation system. My hope is for someone to stand up and shout:

"IT'S OK TO LEAVE THE PLANTATION!"

Big brother Edward and Mason at Grandfather's house

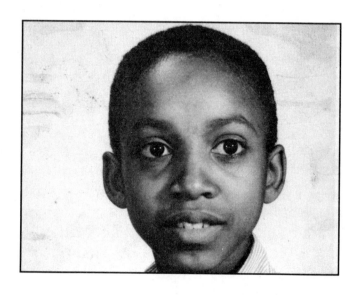

11 years old-1961--Moved from the city to the country

18 years old - graduating from boot camp 1968

Marcella & Waverly Weaver Jr., Mason's Parents

Chapter Two

Wisdom Comes Not From the Journey, But From the Experiences Along the Way

"Only a fool starves in the land of plenty"
Attributed to Rev. Waverly Weaver Jr.

Before the Navy, before Berkeley and before work, came the family. It affected my values and my character. Even when I did not follow the moral teaching of my family, I knew when I was not. I learned a lot from my family and it gave me much strength in those early adult years.

I guess we are all a product of our home environment. This is especially true of young adults. When you are twenty years old, most of your experiences in life have been those of a child. You have had very few experiences as an adult, so you fall back on the adults of your childhood. The structure of your childhood and adolescence will affect how you react to certain situations.

My mother was raised in a traditional family of eight children. Her father laid down moral direction for the children, and her mother enforced it. By the time she was 19, my mother found herself divorced and the mother of two children, both under two and a half years of age.

These two children were my older brother and I, and we found ourselves living with her father in a large home in St. Louis, Missouri. We were the only grandchildren and well supervised. You see, this was also the home of

21

great-grandparents, grandparents, three aunts, and constant visits by our three uncles. Life was fun, and we felt protected and loved. My brother and I were the center of attention for both entertainment and training.

I say training because we were expected to understand the family, with its pride and self-discipline, and to be in control of ourselves. Discipline was primarily handled by the women of the family--my grandmother, mother and aunts. This would include corporal punishment as well as other punishments. The limits that we had were very clearly outlined to us and we were seldom surprised by being punished. We knew which activities would result in punishment and which would not. We learned early either not to do it or not to get caught. Nevertheless, once we were discovered, punishment was expected, and neither argument nor excuse would ward it off. My grandmother used to say: "Oh, you have earned this one, boy! Come here!"

But there are some things that a parent cannot teach. Those things nature must teach. I remember my grandparents' big Black potbellied stove in the kitchen. It was used for heat in the winter and I hated winter; therefore, I spent many mornings close to this stove. When I was two years old, my mother and grandmother would warn me about that stove. "Hot!" "That stove is hot!" "You'd better watch out!" I knew what heat was and I knew it would consume things, but I had no real concept of this thing called *"HOT"* until Mother Nature introduced me to it.

One morning I accidentally brushed against that hot potbellied stove and immediately understood what this *"HOT"* everyone was talking about was. After my introduction to hot, I would warn anyone who got near that stove: "Hot, hot, you'd better stay away!" "The stove is hot!" That was a lesson only nature could teach me, and a few years later it became a lifesaving lesson.

When I was six years old, my brother and I were playing in the attic, which was on the third floor of our home. We had recently gone to the carnival, where it was "Fire Safety Week." The nice fireman had told us about fire safety and cautioned us about opening a "*HOT*" door. He said if we were leaving a burning building, we should check every door before we opened it by using the back of our hands to feel for heat. If we felt *"HOT,"* we were not to open that door.

While we played in the attic, one of the adults sounded the fire alarm. All we heard was: "**FIRE, FIRE**, everyone get out of the house, there is a **FIRE**!" Then my aunt's voice came from the floor below: "You kids get out; the attic is on fire!" As we ran down the hallway to the stairs, we considered going out the back door which led directly down three flights of steps to the backyard. When we got to the closed door, I remembered what the fire captain had said about checking the door. I placed the back of my hand on the door and felt a lot of heat and remembered that old potbellied stove. I immediately took my brother's hand and told him there was fire in that room and we must go out through the front.

If my parents had simply protected me from that pot-bellied stove, I would have been unprotected from the dangers of that fire. Often, in compassion and care, we protect people from harm and leave them open to dangers. The instincts to protect must be balanced with the need for learning. The experiences of life may have saved my life that day, and the warnings of my mother could not have given me what I needed while facing that door.

Soon after the fire, our family went their separate ways. It was not because of the fire, but marriages, military, and other obligations resulted in the family moving out of that great home. We all had to find other places to live and we were sorry to see everyone go. No one was hurt, but I could not help but be thankful for that early lesson nature taught me about fire. It was much better to be taught about "*HOT*" by that old potbellied stove than by the fire in that back room.

That old house was full of love and affection, as were the children. Everyone felt it was his/her responsibility to help train and prepare us for life. I do not remember any speeches about how tough life was or how many obstacles there were going to be.

I Remember Nothing About Giving Up, Or Restrictions Based On My Color. The Only Limits I Remember Were Based On My Age and Position In the Family.

I believe these clearly defined limits gave me more control of my life because I could relax in the wide boundaries the family gave me, always secure and never confused on my limits. This living arrangement was great for my brother and myself. Being the only grandchildren in this big and influential family was especially significant around Christmas and other holidays, but not necessarily for my mother. She needed a place of her own to continue her family. After five years, she remarried, and we moved out of grandpa's home in the city and found our way out to the country.

My new father was very similar to my grandfather. He was a disciplined, hard-working man who did not speak much. He expected a lot from everyone, as well as himself, and he led by example. I can remember many nights when he would come home from working in the steel factory fifty miles away in St. Louis. He would then stay up all night studying for his correspondence school and working in his garden to provide fresh vegetables for us.

Work was his motto, his creed, and his measurement of self-worth. He had left school early to help his family survive on the farm in Arkansas. Nevertheless, he did not let his lack of formal education stop him from telling us how important it was for us. He would always say that employers pay for "knowledge," not just ability. Moreover, while someone could have the ability to build a house (all of the equipment and tools), without the knowledge to do so he would be useless. Gaining knowledge about anything was his passion. He has been one of the wisest men in my life.

That passion for knowledge passed on to his seven sons and one daughter, who have earned a total of two master's degrees and three bachelor's degrees, as well as successful jobs. One son is responsible for uranium management and production planning for a uranium fuel fabricator. Another became a real estate developer. Two became schoolteachers, another has a radio program, and another manages a restaurant. One of his sons is a police officer in St. Louis, and another is an experienced mechanic for a national chain of auto repair facilities. The college degrees were obtained by the use of very few government programs, and a lot of self-determination and discipline.

Looking back on my childhood, I guess one could say we were poor, but we did not know it at the time. My mother and father raised eight kids in a two-bedroom home that they paid for over the span of twenty-five years.

The Child-Rearing Style Of My Parents Would Be "Limits Without Limiting Potential, Punishing Only When It Would Help Us Grow, and Loving Us So We Could Love Ourselves"

Until recently, my mother always stayed home with the children (she did not even get her driver's license until she was thirty-five). She spent so much time at the elementary school and helped us with so much homework that the school started asking her to help out as a teacher's aide. Although she was a "big city girl," she learned to sew, can foods and clean fish (well, not too much fish cleaning!). When we moved from St. Louis to the country, all of us had to hold our own and help. We were all expected to "find" responsibilities, rather than wait until someone "gave" them to us.

The issues of race and relationships with White people were only taught to us as a warning. This was before the civil rights movement, and many of my relatives felt and remembered segregation and discrimination from personal experiences. They warned us about going certain places and our behavior when there, but never instilled any fear or guilt for being Black. I never felt inferior or powerless as a Black child.

My grandfather was a well-known minister and a leader within national organizations. His wife was also a very articulate and powerful woman who was very well respected in the community. Their children grew up to enter relationships that reflected their inner confidence and determination. My Uncle Milford, a scientist, spent 27 years in the U.S. Army, retired as Lieutenant Colonel and afterwards obtained a Ph.D. One of his younger brothers, Samuel, is a college instructor in California; his other brother, Alvah, retired after 39 years as a schoolteacher. I could also find no reason for failure from my aunts. Aunt Carolyn was a nurse, Aunt Marilyn was a caseworker supervisor for the Department of Social Services, and my Aunt Doris retired as the Director of Voter Registration for St. Louis County. Aunt Geraldine, a noted seamstress, died at an early age. I was expected to learn and I was expected to go as far as I wanted, not as far as someone would let me go. In my family, there is a difference between failure and not trying, and failure is preferred.

I always knew I could accomplish something with my life. Accomplishment was always taught by example and instruction. At family reunions, one of my uncles would always recite the family history for all to hear. This sense of pride shielded me from the defeatist attitudes I would experience later in life. I guess I looked at myself as a "Vaughn" because that was my grandfather's name. All of my experiences as a Black child were those of a "Vaughn." I did not know what is was to be a "Black" person but I did know what it was like to be a "Vaughn." That is the attitude I took with me when my new father moved us to this small, predominantly White community—a community where some of the residents had a different understanding of what Black people should act like. The cultural shock was not with my family; it was with them.

That Town and I Went Through A Lot Of Changes While I Lived There. From 1961 Until 1968, We Clashed Over What Type Of Man I Would Become

It was a clash over the values my family had versus the stereotypes some in this community had. My experiences with this small town ended on April 4, 1968. On that day Dr. Martin Luther King was killed, and it was the day I joined the United States Navy.

It is nice to get home occasionally to reflect on the past and plan the future. This town has gone through many changes since I left for the Navy in 1968, but in some ways it remains virtually unchanged. The population is still near 6,000 and it still has the rural innocence that I remember. Fishing is still good and our basketball team continues to be a power to reckon with in the conference.

However, the children I left behind have children of their own, and the face of the town has been altered. You can still tell the strangers in town because they are the ones locking their car doors while shopping on Main Street.

My parents and all of their neighbors still sleep with unlocked doors and no bars on the windows. You can look hard, but still find no graffiti anywhere. People still nod hello to you because they think you must be a neighbor. The library will still allow you to check out a book without a card, if you have family living there.

When my family moved there in 1961, we were the first new Black family in a long time to arrive. The town's population was segregated and both Black and White residents knew their places and accepted the way things were. The local bus cafe just began to serve meals to Black people, but you did not feel welcome, and the only cab company did not serve our community. Black residents were only allowed to swim in the local creek, not at the beautiful recreation center just out of town. I can remember going into the local theater to see a movie, only to be reprimanded by the usher for sitting in the "White" section.

The Black section consisted of the last three rows on the left aisle. If the movie was a good one (and it had to be for us to go there) and the last three rows filled up, we had to sit on each other's laps. I accepted this (at 12 years old) until I was forced to sit on a stranger's lap to watch a movie. I vowed never to enter that theater again and I never have.

Insulting names and derogatory comments were common and accepted in this community. My big brother and I found ourselves in a strange world where people could smile and be friendly one moment and then speak the most vile things to you the next.

Looking back at these times, I understand that their reactions and beliefs were more learned than anything else. I do not think that it was a racist town, but it had plenty of racist people living there.

I do not want anyone to misunderstand my memories of this town. It was by far an overwhelmingly positive experience. Hunting, fishing, exploring caves, playing baseball and winter ice skating on the creek were all part of my growing up. Where else can you pick out your Christmas tree in the summer while playing in the woods and retrieve it in December?

What changed this town were the people, not government. It was education, not programs. Now there is no Black section of town, no White-only businesses and no open discrimination. This town is working out the problems of the past because it must. They have no gangs, few illegal drugs, no real crime, and a clean environment. It is still a place to call home. It is my history and it is always nice to be home.

What changed this town into what it is today were the people of decency and honor speaking out and forcing the ignorant and cruel people to back away. It was not government programs that opened the swimming pool to Blacks. No agent of the Federal government forced the community to accept Blacks living on the other side of the tracks. What changed this community was the community itself.

Children who grew up with each other entered adulthood wondering why their classmates could not shop or live with them. This community recognized that good and bad people come in all colors and cultures. In this small town we were too close to remain strangers. We had to become neighbors.

I qualified to graduate high school as a junior because I had completed all of the academic classes. When questioned by the school counselor, I informed him of my intention to enter college. This kind and gentle man whom I had known for years looked at me with compassion and understanding. He put his hand on my back and expressed his concern in a sympathetic manner. *"Mason, why try to get into college? All you would do is take a seat from a more deserving White person. Let me call down to the shoe factory and see if I can get you a job with the other colored boys."*

He believed that Black people did not belong in higher education and he refused to let me graduate with the senior class. I honestly believe he thought he was doing me a favor. I had resigned myself to stay in school and play basketball another year.

About one week later, I was descending the steps to the gym when I heard the coach and another player discussing the potential starters for next year, and my name came up. The coach was saying he would use me often but never start me because *"I will never have another Black player take a scholarship away from you guys again."* I approached the coach and informed him I was not coming back for my senior year and would finish high school in the military.

What gave me the courage to disregard the defeatist attitude of the counselor and the negative outlook of the coach was a strong family, not a strong government program. How could the counselor convince me I could not go on to college when I had three uncles with college degrees? My mother was attending the same college while he was saying how hopeless it was for me.

Because my family taught by example, I did not waver at this attempt to redirect my life. Success begins with the family, which is why our families are under such attack by the Plantation Mentality.

Years later I was visiting and saw the counselor in town. I said hello, took his hand and thanked him. He looked confused and inquired why I was thanking him. I explained that I had three college degrees, and owed much to him. As he looked even more puzzled, I continued to explain.

I left this small town and joined the Navy. I became disabled and was forced to enter college with severe injuries. While on pain medication and unable to walk or sit down for long periods, I struggled through college. I had often thought of him and his doubts of me. Every time I was up late and in pain with more chapters to read, I would think of him. When I had to choose between relieving my pains with medication or staying alert in class, I would think of him. When I felt overburdened and wanted to quit, I would think of him. He was a true motivator.

The only options I gave myself were getting through it or calling him to see if he still had contacts at the shoe factory. I thanked him for giving me so much to prove— not to him, but to myself.

You see, long before I came under the influence of the coach and school counselor, I had been under the influence of my family. Long before I was discouraged by these experts smiling in my face, I had been fully motivated by example and deed. They could not get me to accept their opinions of me because my opinion was forged by a deep self-confidence given to me by a strong family.

Once the slave master takes away the importance of the family, he becomes the new family and authority in the community. We must recommit ourselves to strong families so our children can fight off the subtle attacks by the spirit of that coach and counselor.

Chapter Three

A Historical Perspective

"If there be those who would not save the Union unless they could at the same time destroy slavery, I do not agree with them. My paramount object in this struggle is to save the Union, and is not either to save or destroy slavery. If I could save the Union without freeing any slave, I would do it; and if I could save it by freeing all slaves, I would do it; and if I could do it by freeing some and leaving others alone, I would also do that. What I do about slavery and the colored race, I do because it helps to save this Union."
Abraham Lincoln in a letter to Horace Greeley
August 22, 1862 [1]

After I joined the Navy, I had until June 11, 1968, to report for duty. Therefore, I sat at home watching the riots and destruction that followed the death of Dr. King. Rebellion spread in over a hundred U.S. cities, and soon the death toll was climbing. In Washington, D.C., Chicago, and other locations across America, it was the beginning of a long hot summer.

It took over twenty thousand Federal troops and thirty-four thousand National Guardsmen to confront the rebellion. Schools were canceled and even the start of Major League Baseball was postponed.

Most young men face uncertainty days before joining the military while their country is at war. I faced additional anxiety because my country seemed to be at war with herself.

Finally, on June 11, 1968, I left for boot camp and the real world disappeared for 11 weeks. A few days earlier, on June 8, 1968, a man named James Earl Ray had been arrested for the assassination of Dr. King. I thought that would cool things off, that justice was going to be served and all would be well.

Boot camp was so regulated that hardly any news filtered in. I did not hear about the arrest of one hundred citizens at the closure of "Resurrection City." That happed on June 24 that year, long after I had left for camp. The July race riots in Cleveland, Ohio, and Gary, Indiana, were not reported to us. I had other things to worry about; I was in a new world far from home. It was a world that had every intention of putting me in harm's way and I was concentrating on learning as much about surviving in that world as possible.

I had to learn how to stop a flooding compartment, put out a boiler room fire and many other new things a country boy needed to know for sea duty. I was busy learning the new language and new world of the Navy. However, the day Dr. King died will remain one of the most unforgettable dates in my memory.

While I was in the Navy, I met many people from all over the country, sailors from every walk of life and every economic level. For the first time in my life, I realized that there were people who had a different point of view of race relations than I did. My whole family structure was challenged by this new environment and I felt the need to justify my beliefs.

The civil rights movement was in full gear and many of the Black sailors began to express themselves along racial lines. I was curious about this. Who was I as a person? Who was I as a man and what was my country? Instead of following the rhetoric of the times, I decided to study my history. Because I dropped out of school needing only one class to graduate, I took history at a local school.

The instructor turned out to be a radical Black revolutionary and turned the class into a study of "Black history" in America. It was the best class I had ever experienced and it started an eagerness in me to learn more about myself and my people.

Many students were looking for reasons to blame White America for problems within the Black community. I was looking for reasons to be proud of what we had accomplished in spite of the problems. We both found what we were looking for.

The Slave Trade and the Black American

No one could deny the absolute cruelty of the slave trade. Slavery forced nine generations to develop self-hatred, little respect for families, little care for education, and general hopelessness. I choose to give more time and credibility to the success of Black Americans despite the burdens of slavery.

I Am Not a Victim — I Am Victorious!

There have not been people of any nation, during any time, who have suffered as much as did the Black Americans under slavery, as well as afterwards. However, despite laws that made it illegal to read and write, despite laws forbidding ownership of property, despite families separated by selling and buying, Black people not only survived slavery in America, but we have thrived!

Africa was also colonized by the same force that brought slavery to America. Africans suffered just as much as did the Black Americans. Something happened to the continent that resulted in its warriors becoming helpless to the European invasion. What happened to a continent impenetrable by foreign armies, unbending to cultural influences and unwavering to any outside pressure to change?

I asked myself this question and so should you. Once I found the answer, I found the reason for the slave trade and the reason for the demise of the African continent. Know your past so you can control your future.

When the Mali King Mansa Musa's pilgrimage entered Cairo in July of 1324, he came with 60 to 100 camels loaded with gold, and an estimated 60,000 people. Surely, the European travelers saw this splendid display of gold and word of this rich African kingdom got back to Europe. So why did the Europeans, 150 years later, travel all the way across the Atlantic looking for "El Dorado" when there was so much gold 500 miles away in Africa? Why didn't they run over Africa like they did the Indians of South America? Maybe it was for the same reason Rome conquered only the coastal countries of Africa and not the interior. Maybe they knew their history. Why was the slave raiding primarily on the coast and not inland? The answer is that the inland slave trade was accomplished by negotiations and treaties with tribal chiefs.

Not only did the interior of Africa have gold and camels, but also they were protected by a well-armed, highly motivated, and disciplined army. This army had already defeated the same Muslim army that conquered Portugal and Spain. They had a reputation of fiercely defending their land from invaders. The prospects of venturing into Africa and dealing with the African warriors persuaded the Europeans to consider going to South America.

We, the descendants of the tribes taken out of Africa, fought and won our freedom and have successfully begun the journey to equality on the land where we once were held as slaves. We have achieved more with less than any people in the history of mankind, and we should be proud of it.

After all of the hardships and 125 years of post-slavery bigotry, we are the wealthiest, best-educated, healthiest, most influential Black people on this planet. No African nation can claim the educational or political influence of Black Americans. No Caribbean Island can compare with the health of Black Americans. No country from Brazil to Britain can show as many Black people on their Supreme Court, in Congress, as Nobel Prize winners, or world-recognized entertainers.

When I ask some of these self-proclaimed "victims" where else they would rather be a Black person, someone always mentions countries like Britain or Sweden. Of course, when I ask them if they can remember the last British judiciary member who was Black, or the last Swedish legislator who was Black, they cannot answer. I do not know if there have ever been any such members, but the fact is that we have done more in this country for African people and ourselves than Africa has done for itself. Let us stop being ashamed of our success. Since we cannot go back and correct the wrongs of the past, let us go forward and establish the accomplishments of the future.

All of the current "African pride" movements are fashion statements of no real economic or social value. If one would look at the achievements of Black people on both continents, it seems to me that Africans should be imitating Black Americans. Black Americans lead the world in almost every field: from entertainment to politics, from Colin Powell's effective leadership of the world's greatest military (40% Black Americans), to United Nations ambassadors. Black Americans have thrived!

Since 1444 When the First Portuguese Sailors Took Slaves Out Of Africa, Black People Have Been Hampered With A Huge Inferiority Complex

It may be quite understandable, since generation after generation was beaten, raped, killed, sold, and otherwise punished for showing the slightest bit of self-esteem. For nine generations it was against the law to learn to read and write. It was against the law to look another man in the eye and speak your mind, or even to defend yourself and your property. Legal beatings were given to Black people for speaking in the wrong tone of voice or failing to move fast enough. It became a survival technique to deny one's own dignity. Mothers raised their children not to "act smart" or express themselves in a positive manner. The whole community of slaves suffered for the actions of any one of them. There was great community pressure to remain in one's "place." You could not bring any attention to the group. How one acted around the master could bring "credit to the race" and was encouraged.

Black men were an additional benefit if they made babies. He did not have to worry about taking care of his family, raising his kids, or caring for his woman. If he were successful at breeding, he would be loaned out to other plantations solely to make more babies. Today we have far too many Black men "bragging" about all of their babies from different women.

The slave system was very well organized. The master was the plantation owner and controlled the means of existence for everyone on the plantation. His slaves were worked by White hired help known as "slave overseers." These men rode the fields on horseback, with their whips poised to administer immediate punishment if the slave did not work fast or hard enough. The slave overseer was also the "first response" team to chase after runaway slaves. Since they were always on horseback and on patrol, they usually were the ones who intercepted the slaves who had not escaped the plantation. There were special hunters for the slaves who made it off the plantation.

Then the slave driver was a slave who the master put in charge of a work group, field, the big house, or over the entire plantation. His job was to keep everyone working and afraid of the master. He was treated better than other slaves and could feel free to approach Master with questions and give information. The slave driver's job and status would be in great jeopardy if slaves started escaping the plantation. Therefore, it was in his best interest to maintain the status quo to keep his position and his life.

The slave system allowed only one day of the week for slaves to have for themselves, and that day was Sunday. The only time slaves could meet privately in large groups, without a White person present, was at the church meeting on Sunday morning. Consequently, most slave revolts and uprisings were planned by the ministers or church groups. Because of fear and mistrust of the slave driver, overseer and others, most planned rebellions on the plantation were reported to the master by someone else in the slave community. This caused resentment and mistrust amoung the slaves and secured the plantation for the master. The plans for rebellion or escape were usually "sold out" for scraps of meat or very small privileges. This is where the term "sellout" came from.

The master kept the slaves in such need that the slaves' very survival depended on preying on their own people. This sounds like the inner-city Black on Black crimes of today. The fact that we still eat garbage thrown away by the master and scrounged by the slaves speaks to the depth of the degradation. After the master slaughtered a pig, he took everything he wanted and discarded the rest. The slave, so deprived of meat, had to find ways to make food out of the garbage. Do you think we naturally developed a taste for the pig's guts, feet, ears, tails, nose, neck or other parts not to be mentioned? Even the fat off the pig's back was used to survive, and survive they did. They not only survived, but they prepared for their day of freedom, and they hoped for a day of dignity. We owe it to our ancestors to take full advantage of every opportunity we have. If they survived on the garbage of the master, surely we can survive with the legal right to compete.

The Black ministers held a degree of respect from the slave masters, and they were allowed to speak to the master on behalf of the slaves. The Black ministers assume the same status today. How many civil rights leaders have been ministers? Why does the news media always go to the Black churches for comments on how the Black community feels about a certain subject? The Black churches have historically been either social rooms or war rooms. They were planning either the community picnic and food drive or a march downtown and a business boycott. From Nat Turner, as a slave with a vision to be like Moses, to Martin Luther King's dream, Black ministers have been the focal point of the Black expression.

While the slaves knew they were helpless and had to cooperate to survive, they still had hope. They had found a new religion and embraced it. It was a religion of salvation and its lessons were filled with verses like: "Let my people go," "He who calls on the name of the Lord will be saved," and others that gave hope. There is no real evidence that the slaves believed that "Servants be obedient to thy master" was God's endorsement of their plight. There were over 250 slave revolts and rebellions recorded up to the Civil War. (2) Black people found hope in the Bible, not hopelessness. It was this hope that inspired prayer and kept them alive. It was their dream that one day their offspring would not have to worry about being sold, beaten, or killed. It was the seemingly hopeless dream that one day it would not be against the law to teach their children to read and write.

They waited generation after generation, and after hundreds of years of degrading, socially crippling activities, freedom finally came. The slaves were finally free and able to leave the plantation. Finally, they could form real families, educate their own children, and create their own society. However, after four hundred and twenty years of surviving by not showing intelligence, and after four hundred and twenty years of a community discouraging its members to achieve, and after four hundred and twenty years of depending on someone else for basic human needs, Black people found it hard to leave the plantation.

There were great success stories even before slavery ended. Many Black slaves defied the community and the master by learning to read and write and became very successful. However, the overwhelming numbers of slaves were happy to remain on the plantation or to move north to the new plantations called "factories" in the major cities. The Civil War ended in 1865, but Black Americans had to wait one hundred more years to exercise any real civil freedoms in this country.

After One Hundred Years, Black Americans Still Had Not Left the Plantations

We still could not move into the neighborhoods of our choice, vote, run for office, use public restrooms, or even eat in restaurants. We still had a fear of the slave master, overseer, and the slave driver. They were still in the community doing the same job. The masters were the politicians who claimed control over the South after the Civil War. They were the ones with all the power; they were the ones you had to approach. The slave drivers were "social" and even "religious" leaders in the Black community. Their job was to play power broker and get services for the community from the master. These services included welfare, sharecropping jobs, low-paying domestic jobs in the city, and minimal health care. Again, this new system of plantation life had its Black breeder. The system discouraged Black men to be in the home with their babies because welfare and other "aid" would be shut off. The young under-educated Black women were encouraged to have more babies because their aid and services would be increased. Therefore, you had a system where Black men were bragging about "all" the babies they had all over town. Black women were hanging out of tenement windows on the 1st and 15th of the month looking for "my" check.

Before the Civil War, there were nine generations of slaves taught to hate and distrust themselves. They could not read or write and had no defense against the system. Now we have four, five, or six generations of Black people on welfare with no motivation. Our school systems have not taught reading or thinking skills. We still congregate on urban plantations lacking many services. We still turn to the slave driver to go to the master for us, hoping to get little things we need.

Of course, Master will give us the little things we need, as long as we vote the right way and follow our overseer's instructions. The Black community still exercises control over its members who try to "make it" without the overseer's blessing. They are called "Uncle Tom," "Handkerchief head," "Sellout," or many other names that are reserved for Black Americans who move to the wrong side of town, speak proper English, or decide to marry despite color.

On the plantation, the slaves had to watch out for the "sellout" (who would disclose the plans of the slaves to the master for a little scrap of meat). Master still pays for these services, but the real "sellouts" of today are the Black leaders who are selling us into a life of poverty and degradation while making millions providing "services" for us.

The Real "Sellouts" Are Those Black

Americans Who Try To Keep Others Down By Looking At Themselves As Victims

Those Black people, who are trying to keep you from speaking the English language, getting education instead of recreation, competing instead of complaining and actually dreaming of a better life instead of resigning yourself to poverty and hopelessness, are the "sellouts."

These new "sellouts" are very smart. They actually talk as if they are not the "sellouts." Like their namesakes of old, these "sellouts" are among us, pretending to be our friends while they are doing the master's job. They are the ones who are always ready for a demonstration against someone who does not like them. They never show the motivation to compete against them, only to complain about them. They want you to be angry but never motivated. They want you to follow them instead of your dreams. They treat Black people as if we are a group of retarded individuals who need their care and concern. We cannot act without them, vote, or even go to school without their input. What an insult to the intelligent, hardworking, achieving Black people who have built this great nation. (Should Black Americans who didn't let Jim Crow, the Ku Klux Klan, White Citizens Council, racist police and judges, red lining, little education, and less hope rob them of their dignity be expected to depend upon White America for guidance?) We are a nation of achievers and survivors, and the overseers do not want you to know it because then you would not need their leadership.

Martin Luther King was a Black leader, and I respect and honor the sacrifice he made. However, when he died his dream almost died with him. Why? Because once you have a nation of followers behind one leader, you can simply cut off the leader and the people will perish. What if we had 20-30 million leaders? How can you stop that?

The current "Black leaders" are ineffective, paralyzed, and impotent contributors to Master's plantation. All they do is preach that we are victims and they are leading us to salvation and prosperity. They are leading you to their prosperity, not yours. They will not tell you that the civil rights movement has been won! You are now free to compete in America and win! There will always be people around who will not like you or give you a break, but the civil rights movement was about giving you the right to compete. Take advantage of that right!

Today the civil rights movement has made great progress. We can not only vote, but we can win political office. There are Black governors, mayors, police chiefs, district attorneys, doctors, members of Congress, senators, and business people. We no longer need to wonder if Black people will be seen in positive roles in the movies, because we now make movies.

Everything Black people "think" they can do, they do better than anyone on the planet. We "think" we can play basketball, do we not? We "think" we can play baseball, football, or box, do we not? We "think" we can sing, dance and entertain, do we not? We even "think" we can shoot, kill, rob, and sell dope, do we not? If you put the top Black basketball, football, or baseball players on the same team, no other combination of players would beat them. Just look at the U.S. basketball team in the past Olympics. The top entertainers in music, acting, TV, comedy, or dancing will always include—Black people. Why? What about racism? What about the "conspiracy to keep the Black man down?"

Charley Pride was not afraid of racism when he became the Country and Western singer of the decade. He was singing in honky-tonk bars in Mississippi and Alabama while Black people were being lynched, and he still made it. Giving up a baseball career, he entered the "White man's" field, where even his own people discouraged him.

Jack Johnson did not care about a White conspiracy when he became the first Black heavyweight boxing champion. He was knocking out White men while they were beating Black men for looking the wrong way. It was dangerous for him to enter certain towns, let alone enter the ring. He did not let the hatred, bigotry or fear stop him.

Do you think Jackie Robinson let other people (White or Black) stop him from breaking into baseball? After so many years of witnessing Jim Crow at its worst, Robinson responded by thriving in everything he did. He not only thought he was equal, but dared to believe he was better. We will always have someone not wanting us to succeed, because they just may not want the competition.

Black Americans have many reasons to stand proudly. We not only survived slavery, we have thrived! Despite all of the harshness of the slave system, Black people in this country are the wealthiest, best educated, most influential Black people on the planet. We ran the strongest military in the world, and we sit on the Supreme Court of the most valued legal system the world has ever known. The everyday activities of our celebrities are followed worldwide. The influence and power of Black Americans had as much to do with the freeing of Nelson Mandela as the efforts of his own people. Black people in America can be proud of what they have achieved here. Again, ask yourself the question: where else would I rather be? What other country offers the most opportunity and tradition? There are no African nations, Caribbean islands, or South American countries where Black people have made a better life for themselves.

We owe it to the struggles of our ancestors, the prayers of generation after generation, and the bloody sacrifices of never-to-be-known heroes who knew not to give up on America. If anyone should claim America as its own, it should be Black people. Her land was cleared by us, her people were fed by us, her factories were worked by us and her wars were fought by us. All these were sacrifices for little or no pay, benefits or thanks. We have paid for this country. We have earned the right to be part of it. All we need to do is have the courage to leave the plantation. Do not pay much attention to those who do not want you to make it; they just cannot stand the competition. They see what has happened since Black people entered the fields of entertainment, sports, or any other field they "thought" they could. They do not want the competition. Do not let them stop you.

What if Black people, as a group, thought they could own businesses, buy and develop real estate, or become scientists? Let us leave the plantation knowing it is going to be rough and a struggle. Let us not be afraid of struggles. It is our history to overcome and thrive!

"African American" Versus "Black American"

A few years ago a group of Black Americans gathered to discuss a new American agenda. It was called a convention, and "delegates" formed caucuses and voted on issues. This convention resulted in the term "Afro-American" being changed to "African American." I was not present at this convention, nor was I given the opportunity to vote for a delegate. I have some problems with the term "African American." It still is not descriptive enough for me. A "Mexican American," "German American," or even a "European American" simply describes the country of one's ancestry. It does not describe culture, race or even color.

An "African American" could include White South Africans, German descendants of Western Africa, Egyptians, Moroccans, Libyans, or Arabs, Dutch, Portuguese, etc. I prefer "Black American of Slave descent," which is a description that better identifies me. I know some Black people do not want to be reminded of their slave past, but if we understood our achievements in the face of slavery, we would be more proud and understanding. I could not accept this title of "African American" because it diminished the achievements and contributions of my people to this American culture.

If I moved to Africa, would I become an African American African? If I then return to the United States would that make me an African American African American? How can anyone, including ourselves, take Black people seriously when we cannot even get serious about our name? It is clear that dividing us into hyphenated Americans only keeps more of us dependent and culturally deprived. We must resist this force trying to keep us from celebrating the tremendous success we have achieved here in America.

Black Americans and the Christian Way of Life

The one thing about God that is clear is that God is consistent! What God likes, He likes forever. What God hates is always hated by God and whenever God punishes or rewards a people, He will punish and/or reward other people for the same thing.

On November 18, 1978, more than nine hundred followers of Jim Jones died with him in Jonestown, Guyana. This mass murder-suicide struck very close to home for me. Most of the victims were Black, and a great many had come from the San Francisco area. I had attended college, was working in that area, and had many friends there.

My first question was a racial one because that was how I thought in 1978. How could hundreds of Black people follow this White man anywhere? In addition, the strange behavior he required of these church folks was hard to understand. Here were older individuals who had spent decades in the front pews of the church and still could not recognize this man for the demon he was. To what kind of church did they belong?

I was not a churchgoing Christian at the time, but my upbringing under my father Rev. Weaver and my grandfather Rev. Vaughn made certain things clear. I was not going to let someone else share my wife, I was not going to give everything I have earned to someone else, and I was not going to follow some power-hungry White guy back to the jungles.

Jim Jones was a very popular preacher with the politicians of San Francisco. He was seen often in the company of the city leaders and was given much respect. I found even the Black leaders were accepting of him. Some called it charisma, others attributed it to his ability to build up a large congregation; I call it "birds of a feather flocking together." However, I had what I believed was a natural suspicion of a White leader of a Black congregation, one whose father was or had been a Ku Klux Klan member! Jim Jones did not pledge any following of his father, and publicly rejected the philosophy of the Klan. However, this one man probably caused more death, destruction and misery on the Black community than the entire history of the Klan.

Because I had worked for Congress and, at the time of the deaths, was working for the U.S. Department of Energy, many of the relatives and friends of victims called on me for advice and information.

Congressman Rand's inquiry into the cult's activities had sparked the mass suicide. It also sparked in me a fear of not knowing who God was. That event and others began the most important research project I had ever embarked upon. Finding the truth about religion and my relationship with my creator became very important.

When I saw the people of God in the Old Testament, I noticed every time they disobeyed God and turned against Him, they went into slavery. Every time they turned to God and repented, they came out of slavery. I can find no example in the Bible or secular history where the people of God went into slavery worshiping God. They may have come out of slavery worshiping God, but God's people never entered slavery while obeying Him.

So, with that in mind, I began to look at the history of Black people in Africa and guess what I found? Through queens like Candace and Nefertari and kings like Solomon, Africans had a rich knowledge of God. And while they worshiped Him they flourished. But soon division and delusion came, and they stopped worshiping the Creator and started worshipping the creation. Then false religions came in and the people left God. The people became so weak; the Europeans just walked into Africa and took what they wanted. Africa was not conquered by a great war. Africans were weakened by spiritual and social decay, not by military might.

Black people were taken in chains from Africa while they were still worshiping a false god. Many African countries were colonized while they Worshiped this false god. Then something started to happen in America. First, the slaves began to accept Jesus Christ as their Savior, and a movement began among Christians of America called "the Abolition Movement." Black churches sprung up on plantations and through this movement slavery was finally lifted. Again, when God's people turned to Him, they were delivered.

Immediately after slavery, Black people achieved many things and were generally prosperous. In the early 1930's, we started leaning back toward that same false god who we came here with. Since then, our community has fallen apart again. If you are a Black American, or anyone interested in what keeps a people free, then learn your history. If you are an American interested in how Americans can stay free, understand history (or "HIS STORY")! Whenever a nation turns from God, they go into slavery or destruction. When they turn to God, they are delivered by God.

Look at God's chosen people (read Judges chapters 2 through 6). Whenever they turned from God, they went into captivity. When they turned to God, they were freed. Repeatedly, the people of God were safe only when they honored God. Look at modern history. Palestine was in the hands of ungodly people for hundreds of years. They did not serve the true God, and their land was a desert wasteland. In other countries God's people were praying to get their homeland back, and when God delivered them back to their land (the same land), have you noticed what happened? The same desert wasteland that the ungodly had for hundreds of years has (in less than 40 years) become an oasis, green and productive. God turned the desert into farm land for those who love Him.

The study of religion is a very important question, a question that must be answered with truth and understanding. It has eternal consequences and should be the most important question a nation, community, or individual should ask. When I grew into manhood and had to face this question I came to a crossroad between Allah and the God of the Bible. It was resolved very fast once I considered the history.

The followers of Allah controlled the Promised Land for 700 years. Apparently, they worshiped properly and attended to all of the requirements of Allah. So, why was Palestine a desert wasteland for the people? They could not grow enough food to feed themselves. Then, while these people were worshiping Allah, the unbelieving Christians and Jews forced the Muslims out of the promised land. Not only do we have to ask, "Why would Allah allow this," but also, "why would he bring prosperity to the land only one generation later?" The Jews took over the country and in less than 40 years it has become a rich, lush garden, feeding everyone who lives there. Why would Allah allow this?

I Looked Into the History Of the African Worshipers of Allah Who Were Taken Off Their Knees, Chained and Sold Into Slavery

Why would Allah allow his people to enter slavery while Worshiping him, spend hundreds of years calling his name and allow freedom only when they stopped calling his name and began calling on the name of Jesus?

I learned from my Black history classes that the slaves were converted to Christianity and began to pray and have faith in Jesus. Then the abolition movement was started by Christians, and there began a movement of freedom for Black people here. Even the colonized continent of Africa had a similar history. The independence of each nation was preceded by its people's conversion to Christianity. It became obvious that no real God would allow His people to go into slavery worshiping him, and no real God would bring them out of slavery while they worshiped a false God. Even at an early age, I did not know the complete truth—but I did know I could not go back and worship a god who could not keep me out of slavery.

What I did not find was this great connection to the Islam religion that we hear so much about. In the 1960's and 70's I kept hearing about the "Black man's god" and a return to worship him. Well, if this Black man's god was Allah, then why did the prophet Mohammed completely avoid Africa? I cannot find any statement, writings or traditions placing him on the African continent.

The Muslim religion came into Africa by way of war, not by missionaries. It flourished by participating in the slave trade, and continues in fear and violence. Even with its long history in Africa, the Muslim religion has fewer members in Africa than the less-touted Christian religion. I was amazed to see that the estimated number of Christians living in Africa is 327,204,000, but the number of Muslims on the continent was only 278,365,000.[3] I verified this by cross-referencing many sources, including almanacs and world population data.

God has promised to turn to them who turn to Him, to prosper their land, and to be their God (II Chronicles 7:14, I Peter 5: 6 and Ephesians 2:17-19). Therefore, if you are a Christian, you cannot be a "Black Christian." If you are a Christian, you cannot be a "White Christian." If you are truly a Christian, you are a new person and part of the "race of Christ!" (I Peter 2:9-10, II Cor. 5:17) Be wary of all secret attempts that lead us back into the recognition of the hollow pagan rituals that made us weak and vulnerable to the slave masters and oppressors of the past. Worship God! God's way is freedom!

This revelation, that God was consistent for all people and for all times, eventually led me to reevaluate my personal relationship with Him. I had to decide if I was worshiping God the way God requires or my way. I had left the God of my grandfather and my father and turned to youthful foolishness. However, because of the love of God I saw in their lifestyle, I sought Him again. Thank God for faithful parents!

Chapter Four

The Plantation Mentality: Our Journey From Victim to Victorious!

"Not only do I pray for it, on the score of human dignity, but I can clearly foresee that nothing but the rooting out of slavery can perpetuate the existence of our union, by consolidating it in a common bond of principles."
George Washington

One thing I learned about history is that no one will ever give up power without encouragement from the powerless. I could never understand the constant call for the plantation owner to give us some of his power. It seemed as if we could not learn from history, that freedom is never given, and it must be taken.

I studied the plantation system with great attention to the subtle conditioning of the slaves. There was always an attempt to redirect the slaves' attention from freedom from the plantation to relief in the plantation. Master was always the center of attention and always the source of power. Today we are still looking for the master to solve our problems and accept responsibility over us. Every problem our so-called leaders come up with requires the master's attention and his solution. I decided while in college that if he was the source of my problems, he could not be the answer to my problems. If I learned anything about the plantation system, it was how little I needed it.

Let us Face It, the Plantation Was a Business

Its purpose was to provide profit and prosperity for the owner and his family. It was not for the purpose of helping poor Whites, slaves, or the nation. It was for profit, power, and culture. Like any other business, the plantation followed a set business principle: reduce cost and increase profit. The biggest cost to the plantation was the slave; the slave was also its tool for profit.

When the abolitionists began to stir the consciousness of America and the Civil War loomed upon the horizon, the plantation owners began to realize that one day the slaves would leave the plantation. They began to devise ways to keep the slaves dependent on the owners of the plantations and at the same time have a belief that they were free and independent. The slave master had to replace his system of "overseers, slave drivers and slave breakers" with different names and responsibilities. Their purposes would not change. They would keep the slaves working and producing a profit for the master and his family.

The technique was to spread distrust and mis-education to the slaves in order to make the plantation life seem more attractive than life outside the plantation. Slaves were told to "watch out for them damned Yankees."

Politically, the South had to change from its roots. The party of the slave master began portraying itself as the party that cared about the slaves' well-being. *"We'll take care of you, just trust us."* The slave, now free, again gave his trust to the slave master and his friends, the overseers and slave drivers. Again, the slave depended upon the master for every element of life—including what to think and say.

Suddenly the Black Americans Lost Control of Their Schools, Businesses and Families

The slave master had to change his image in order to control his slaves. He had to declare compassion as he encouraged dependency by the welfare system. Welfare did not mean just payments to a family for basic subsistence; it also included a system to discourage marriage and participation of the male in the raising of his family. Just like the plantation, the slave male was reduced to a breeder with his female. He had no responsibility for the caring or raising of his kids; "master" did that for you. He did not have to educate, protect, feed, provide healthcare or provide a home for his children. Master did that for him, as long as he did not marry the mother or move in with his children. This was called "Aid to Families with Dependent Children," because that is what they wanted: "dependency" of our children and of us.

So, here we are sitting on the front stoop drinking wine and waiting for the next game of basketball. We tell ourselves, "Don't look for a job, because the 'White man' has them all under control" or "Don't go to school, because there isn't any way you can ever get ahead." Nevertheless, we think because they owe us something, we are justified in taking it by force and crime.

Our women are hanging out of tenement windows waiting for "my check" to arrive so they can "take care of business," as if it was business to be on welfare and stretch money to the end of the month.

Now the slave master has reorganized the plantation and the slaves' way of thinking and is back in control. We vote for the party of the slave master more than the party of the abolitionists. We trust the kidnapper, rapist and murderer because he has promised he has changed, but we do not trust those who gave their life for our freedom because the master does not trust them. We have rejected the party of Lincoln, the Emancipation Proclamation, the 13th and 14th amendments to the Constitution, and the party that paid the price for our liberty, politically speaking. Of course, Master didn't appreciate our liberation, but why have we rejected those who helped? We went from slavery, to sharecropping, to ghetto degradation, all led by Master and his plantation mentality. The only way he can win this game is if he can keep us thinking as slaves. As long as we think we need him and his slave drivers, we will listen only to him. The education of the Black population is the greatest fear of the plantation owner. If we understood our power and our threat, we would not only run him off the plantation, but we would own it ourselves.

I believe this is a well-articulated and executed plan to have us contribute to our own decline. I believe the slave master understood that a united slave population was not a benefit to his lifestyle, and he worked against it. I further believe that we are still living under a calculated plan that keeps us distrusting one another and going to the master for leadership.

The following is a copy of a speech given to Southern slave masters hundreds of years ago. It was by a slave consultant who was brought in to help the masters with their "problem" —slaves not wanting to cooperate. His solution was simple: divide and conquer by spreading mistrust among the slaves, and they will keep it going for hundreds of years. Was he correct? Are we still being manipulated by this system? Read it and decide for yourself.

The Slave Consultant's Narrative

This speech was delivered by a White slave owner, William Lynch, on the bank of the James River in 1712.

Gentlemen, I greet you here on the bank of the James River in the year of our Lord one thousand seven hundred and twelve. First, I shall thank you, the gentlemen of the Colony of Virginia, for bringing me here. I am here to help you solve some of your problems with slaves.

Your invitation reached me on my modest plantation in the West Indies where I have experimented with some of the newest and still the oldest methods for control of slaves. Ancient Rome would envy us if my program is implemented. As our boat sailed south on the James River, named for our illustrious King, whose version of the Bible we cherish, I saw enough to know that your problem is not unique. While Rome used cords of wood as crosses for standing human bodies along its old highways in great numbers you are here using the tree and the rope on occasion.

I caught a whiff of a dead slave hanging from a tree a couple of miles back. You are not only losing valuable stock by hangings, you are having uprisings, slaves are running away, your crops are sometimes left in the fields too long for maximum profit, you suffer occasional fires, and your animals are killed. Gentlemen, you know what your problems are; I do not need to elaborate. I am not here to enumerate your problems, I am here to introduce you to a method of solving them.

In my bag here, I have a foolproof method for controlling your Black slaves. I guarantee every one of you that if installed correctly it will control the slaves for at least 300 years. My method is simple. Any member of your family or your overseer can use it.

I have outlined a number of differences among the slaves; and I take these differences and make them bigger. I use fear, distrust, and envy for control purposes. These methods have worked on my modest plantation in the West Indies and it will work throughout the South. Take this simple little list of differences, and think about them. On top of my list is "Age," the second is "Color" or shade, then there is intelligence, size, sex, size of plan-

tations, status on plantation, attitude of owners, whether the slaves live in the valley, on a hill, East, West, North, South, have fine hair or coarse hair, or are tall or short. Now that you have a list of differences, I shall give you an outline of action—but before that I shall assure you that distrust is stronger than adulation; respect or admiration.

The Black slave after receiving this indoctrination shall carry on and will become self-refueling and self-generating for hundreds of years, maybe thousands.

Don't forget you must pitch the old Black vs. the young Black male, and the young Black male against the old Black male. You must use the dark skin slaves vs. the light skin slaves and the light skin slaves vs. the dark skin slaves. You must use the female vs. the male, and the male vs. the female. You must also have your White servants and overseers distrust all Blacks, but it is necessary that your slaves trust and depend on us. They must love, respect, and trust only us.

Gentlemen, these Kits are your Keys to control. Use them. Have your wives and children use them, never miss the opportunity. If used intensely for one year, the slaves themselves will remain perpetually distrustful. Thank you, gentlemen.

University of Missouri-St. Louis Thomas Jefferson Library Reference Department

It is important to the master and his new slave drivers that you stay uneducated and dependent. Do not "act smart" or show any ambition. Moreover, whatever you do, do not show how you can think for yourself.

It is not our nature to feel so insecure; it is not our nature to kill ourselves with drugs, to prostitute our women or to abuse our kids with low self-esteem and poverty.

It is time we stop depending on the man and start competing against the man. It is time we stop believing we need government to take care of us and stand up to take care of ourselves. It is time we determine our own future and our own direction. It is time we join mainstream America because it is our country.

It is OK to believe in yourself. It is OK to have confidence in your own ability. It is OK to love your woman enough to marry her and live with her. It is OK to challenge yourself to fail or succeed on your own. It is OK to leave the plantation!

Stop Whining and Get To Work

The new inner-city plantation is not only physical but also mental. It has a culture all its own and acts like a disease upon the community. We came out of slavery with pride and self-determination and exploded upon America. In the first ten years after the Civil War we had Black Congressmen, Lt. Governors, many business owners, and at least 20 U.S. patents awarded to Black people. One hundred and twenty years later it seems all we can do is wait on "the man" to give us what we need and want.

I was teaching a class on self-esteem in a private Christian school in San Diego, California. The first thing I asked the students was why they need a class in self-esteem? Why is it that Black kids need someone from the community to instruct them on liking themselves?

What I hoped to teach that class was how unimportant it was to try and find someone in history of whom they could be proud. This may come as a shock to you, but I think it is much more important to be proud of something YOU did rather than finding someone in history in which you can take pride.

I taught about "self-pride," pride in something you have done with something you had control over. It is not pride in what your ancestors did 2,000 years ago or how many inventions Black people developed. It will not motivate you one bit if you still think you could not have done it yourself. It starts with self-pride. I asked my students to come up with one thing they were proud of, something they did themselves that they were determined to do well. They soon understood that you could not take pride in something someone else has done. You can only take pride in what you have done.

Taking pride in yourself is the start of self-pride and self-motivation. Once a child has pride in himself or herself, he or she will then become part of the community and a part of its preservation. It becomes harder to use graffiti and violence if you own part of the community.

If a child doesn't feel he or she is part of the community, then there isn't any need to speak to him or her about pride in the community. After the Los Angeles riots, following the Rodney King beating trial of the L.A. police officers, I asked some San Diego youths their thoughts about the violence. They immediately began to express pleasure in the violence and especially the Koreans targeted in some of the violence. They had begun to believe the stereotypes about Korean grocers and felt it was justified to burn down their businesses. They felt the high price they charged for merchandise was just an example of racist pricing against Black people. In general they felt like victims, and the Koreans were the new victimizers.

However, their attitudes changed after further discussions based upon real-life logic and contemplation. I used the example of a foreign-owned store a few blocks from the school that all of the students knew about. It was open from 7 a.m. until midnight most nights and was the only store open that late in the neighborhood. Across the street was another foreign-owned gas station also open late at night, operated by a family of recent immigrants.

The questions I asked them were very simple. If you

burned down those family businesses: (1) Where would your mother go when she needed baby milk at 10 p.m. and (2) How far will you walk to get candy, drinks or anything else you may want on the way to school and (3) How far would your father have to drive to get gas before going to work? After the riots, these businesses are lost and their convenience will be missed.

My young friends thought we (Black people) should own the stores instead of the foreigners. I agreed it would be nice to do that, but I had another question for them. Would they be willing to reside 8 to 10 in a family, in a two-bedroom house, just to make a down payment on the store? Would they be willing to stop hanging out with their friends at the mall and help run the business and keep it open all night? You see, they didn't understand "sacrifice." You cannot get ahead without sacrifice.

If You Are Not Willing To Sacrifice You Are Not Willing To Succeed

Every successful person known has had to sacrifice much to attain his or her goals. We ridicule the bookworm who sacrificed sports, popularity and acceptance in order to study and achieve the goal of going to college. A sports hero will tell you about the sacrifice in practice and discipline in order to achieve their goals. Goals and dreams are different. A dream is something you think would be nice to do, but a goal is something you think you can do. We should turn more of our dreams into goals and then our goals into plans. A plan is something you are doing. Every plan must include a list of sacrifices. What are you willing to pay for your dreams, goals and plans? If you do not know what you will sacrifice, then you do not really know what you want. When a young person talks to me about his/her plans I ask about the sacrifices.

Chapter Five

The Black Conservative Movement:
The next logical step in the
civil rights movement!

Ninety-nine percent of the failures come from people who have the habit of making excuses."
George Washington Carver

I believe Carver was right. Today the Black community controls 99% of the problems we face. We can blame the White man, slavery, poverty, police brutality or unemployment. However, we are in charge of our own education, we elect the politicians and we control our own destiny.

We give far too much credit to White people and the system and far too little credit to ourselves. We continue to allow our schools to turn out slaves for the system, then blame the system. We see drugs in our neighborhoods and blame the White smugglers instead of the Black pushers. We have drive-by shootings and look to the White gun manufacturers and not at the Black triggermen.

We cannot control the White manufacturers or the smugglers, but we can control our children. The civil rights movement was about who would control our children. However, just like the children of Israel who escaped Egypt, some longed to return to Pharaoh. After the civil rights movement was over, many leaders wanted the security of master's control. Some of us have never understood the civil rights movement or the responsibilities of freedom.

There have always been two sides to the civil rights movement: violence and non-violence. From the suffrage movement and Nat Turner to the Abolitionist and Toussant

L'Overture, we have always had a choice in this struggle. If you followed Dr. Martin Luther King's way or Malcolm X's, the choice was still non-violence or violence.

However, today's choices are different and alarming. This nation seems to be dividing itself into violence and passive victims. The violence is toward our own people, and the passiveness is toward those leading us back onto that plantation of hopelessness. The Black community's inability to act on its own interest is directly due to the passive leaders. These leaders are saying, "give us more," "we cannot make it without your help" and "you owe us something."

It is time to evaluate our commitments and our decisions. Thirty years ago we decided government handouts, welfare, job training, and birth control assistance were needed in our community. Well, it is time to check on this noble mission and evaluate its progress. We have faithfully given our vote to one party, and it is time we look at what we have received for our loyalty. We have blindly followed self-appointed leaders in social, economic and political ideology; let us see if it has benefited us.

Planned Parenthood: Genocide In the Black Community

A very good example of smiling faces devastating our Black community is Planned Parenthood and its founder. Was Margaret Sanger (the founder of Planned Parenthood) a friend to the poor, minorities and the helpless? A recent TV program made her out to be a combination of Joan of Arc and Florence Nightingale. But who was she really? What do we really know about this crusader for women's rights?

Information at the local libraries and bookstores is rare and mostly favorable. But a search of the Library of Congress will uncover a wealth of information in her own writings and letters to her contemporaries. A register of Margaret Sanger's papers indicates a woman obsessed with restricting the birth rights of those she described as unfit. She wanted birth licenses to qualified couples and was willing to use "Negro" Doctors and Ministers to influence and control the "Negro" race.(4)

There are also accusations that Margaret Sanger traveled to Germany and was instrumental in developing Hitler's "Final Solution."

As a Black American, I was particularly interested in her *"Negro Project."* It was a well-thought-out plan to use the Black communities' doctors and ministers to win over the support of the community. I could not help but think of Dr. Joycelyn Elders' and Doctor Henry Foster's obsession with condoms and abortions and their dogmatic support of Planned Parenthood.

The results of decades of Planned Parenthood influence in our community can now be measured. Thirty years ago teen pregnancies in our communities were high but under control. According to Jacqueline J. Cissell, director of Social and Cultural Studies for the Indiana Family Institute, 9% of the population (the Black community) is undergoing 44% of the abortions, and our percentage of the population is shrinking.(5) I called Dr. Mildred Jefferson, founder of the Right to Life Coalition, and she believes these figures are accurate. We are committing suicide. It looks like the *"Negro Project"* is in full force.

Margaret Sanger was a prolific writer and authored books and articles explaining her views. She also published the views of her associates and experts.

Her *"The Birth Control Review"* stated in the July-August 1932 edition, "There are other more remote but equally important gains. One is the enhanced respect to be had from the dominant White race. That the Negro must acquire if he is to enjoy the rights and prerogatives he covets. But acquire it he cannot and will not so long as he remains the thriftless, childlike, irresponsible dependent that he is, for such behavior does not command respect." Even in the social climate of 1932, this seems harsh and racist.

Like most racists, Sanger probably convinced herself that she was helping the poor Negro. It sounds like liberals today, always talking about what we need or should have as if we are their pets, or worse.

They talk about peace, love, harmony and open-mindedness, but their action says hatred and genocide. In a paper titled *"A Plan for Peace,"* Margaret Sanger outlined her main objects of something called *"The Population Congress."*

a. To raise the level and increase the general intelligence of population.

b. To increase the population slowly by keeping the birth rate at its present level of fifteen per thousand, decreasing the death rate below its present mark of 11 per thousand.

c. To keep the doors of immigration closed to the entrance of certain aliens whose condition is known to be detrimental to the stamina of the race, such as feebleminded, idiots, morons, insane, syphilitic, epileptic, criminal, professional prostitutes, and others in this class barred by the immigration laws of 1924.

d. To apply a stern and rigid policy of sterilization and segregation to that grade of population whose progeny is already tainted, or whose inheritance is such that objectionable traits may be transmitted to offspring.

e. To insure the country against future burdens of maintenance for numerous offspring as may be born of feebleminded parents, by petitioning all persons with transmissible disease who voluntarily consent

to sterilization.

f. To give certain dysgenic groups in our population their choice of segregation or sterilization.

g. To apportion farmlands and homesteads for these segregated persons where they would be taught to work under competent instructors for the period of their entire lives.

She goes on to outline the taking control over "morons, mental defective, and epileptics." Her plan called for an inventory of "illiterates, paupers, unemployables, criminals, prostitutes, dope-fiends, in order to better place them on the government-run farms and homestead."

These are her own words, not mine. How much more information would the Black community need before becoming suspicious? Just the title of her book, *"Woman and the New Race,"* should clear up every doubt of the most blinded skeptic.

American Weekly's Article Seems to Be Planned Parenthood's Outline To Rid the World of Inferior People.

Article 1. *The purpose of the American Baby Code shall be to provide for a better distribution of babies, to assist couples who wish to prevent overpopulating of offspring and thus to reduce the burdens of charity and taxation for public relief, and to protect society against the propagation and increase of the unfit.*

Article 2. *Birth control clinics shall be permitted to function as services of government health departments or under the support of charity, or as nonprofit, self-sustaining agencies, subject to inspection and control by public authorities.*

Article 3. *A marriage license shall in itself give the husband and wife only the right to a common household and not the right to parenthood.*

Article 4. *No woman shall have the legal right to bear a child, no man shall have the right to become a* *father without a permit for parenthood.*

Article 5. *Permits for parenthood shall be issued by government authorities to married couples upon application, providing the parents are financially able to support the expected child, have the qualifications needed for proper rearing of the child, have no transmissible diseases, and on the woman's part no indication that maternity is likely to result in death or permanent injury to health.*

Article 6. *No permit for parenthood shall be valid for more than one birth.*

Article 7. *Every county shall be assisted administratively by the state in the effort to maintain a direct ratio between the county birth rate and its index of child welfare. When the county records show an unfavorable variation from this ratio the county shall be taxed by the State...the revenues thus obtained shall be expended by the State within the given county in giving financial support to birth control clinics.*

Article 8. *Feeble minded persons, habitual congential criminals, those afflicted with inheritable diseases, and others found biologically unfit should be sterilized or in cases of doubt be isolated as to prevent the perpetuation of their afflictions by breeding.*

As I read the volumes of her writings, I became frustrated and overwhelmed with the sheer quantity of information. I could use up the space of this entire book just quoting Sanger and her friends. However, more frustrating to me are the number of so-called Black leaders silent on this. How much did their silence cost us? How much damage has been done to the mental state of the community from their silence? Now that you know, will your silence add to the pain?

A great source of knowledge and information on Planned Parenthood and its founder can be acquired from

L.E.A.R.N., the Life Education And Resource Network, P.O. Box 1949, South Road Branch, Poughkeepsie, New York, 12601. I am grateful for the help they gave me in researching this topic.

It does not matter that the sins of the past were done out of lack of knowledge--to continue them after awakening is the greater error.

Other documentation includes a copy of the "*Birth Control News*" of May 31, 1931. On the front cover is their emblem that reads ,"Joyous and deliberate motherhood. A sure light in our racial darkness." Was Margaret Sanger a racist? I do not know, but she most certainly was not a saint. I called Planned Parenthood in San Diego to ask what the racial darkness was. I am still waiting for a return call.

Then there is the famous letter to a Doctor Gamble dated 12-10-39. In it Sanger reveals her plan to use ministers but warns, "We do not want word to go out that we want to exterminate the Negro population, and the minister is the man who can straighten out that idea if it ever occurs to any of their more rebellious members." This brought memories of the nine Black churches that recently passed out condoms during church services in Los Angeles.

These nine Black ministers believed they were helping to keep the community safe by "educating" the children how to sin safely. Nine Black churches with thousands of members passed out thousands of condoms, giving fuel to the belief that we are our own worst enemy.

Sanger's statement could be taken two ways. She could be warning against a misinterpretation of their goals. On the other hand, she could be cautioning against discovery of her real goals. One would need to look at other writings and the general principles she put forth for a clearer understanding of her intent.

And to the liberated women who still may think of Margaret Sanger as a role model; I submit to you quotes from her 1934 article in the *American Weekly Magazine.*

There should be enough evidence to say that more needs to be known and understood about this woman and her organization before we ordain her to sainthood. Perhaps Planned Parenthood has recanted her beliefs. Perhaps they have moved into another direction. I have found no evidence of recantations or explanations of these papers. In fact, the volume of documentation that speaks negatively about her is too much for this short book. We need to spend more time looking at the results of groups like this than listening to the great sounding rhetoric of their ideas and goals. Let us take heed of the old story about wolves in sheep clothing and the song about "smiling faces."

The War On Poverty is Over—and Poverty Won

We thought the war on poverty was great! Who can argue with its goals to reduce poverty, feed breakfast to children, and to teach them? Well, we have spent 5 trillion dollars over the past 3 decades to create 60 million dependent, unmotivated, and depressed people. It has not worked and it has made our community a wreck. We should have the courage to say this is killing us with "kindness"; take your kindness elsewhere. Five trillion dollars is more money than this country has spent on all of the wars we have fought put together. The American Revolution, Spanish-American War, Civil War, World War I, World War II, the Korean Conflict and the Vietnam War combined do not equal the financial efforts we have used for the war on poverty. If we can defeat every enemy with less effort, why can we not defeat poverty? Because there is too much money in poverty!

Black people have faithfully given 90% of their support to one political party in the hopes of getting much back in return. It did not matter that this was the party of the old plantation slave masters; it did not matter that we were turning our backs on the party of Lincoln and the Abolitionists. Master said not to worry and that he would take care of us. Moreover, the plantation slave drivers in our community assured us this was the "new Master" and if we just gave him a chance, he would set us free.

No race, culture or nationality in America has ever achieved economic freedom from political means, but we are still trying. Have you ever wondered why the Koreans, Japanese, Arabs or Chinese in our country are not worried about politics as they make economic progress? Why are we looking for the Master to give us anything? He will never give us all he has. But if we compete, we can win all he has—let us compete.

If political power was enough, wouldn't Watts, Compton and the entire South Central Los Angeles area be thriving? After all, we have had a Black man as the most powerful man in the legislature (Willie Brown as Assembly Speaker for 14 years), a Black man as mayor of California's largest city (Los Angeles), a Black mayor of Compton and a Congresswoman (Maxine Waters), all Democrat. This same area was represented in the California State Senate by a Black woman named Diane Watson. If economic power comes just from politics, Watts should be one of the most expensive, safe and clean places to live in the state. However, it is more than politics!

This is why I say the conservative movement is the next logical step in the civil rights movement. The civil rights movement was always about the legal right to work and live in America. It was never about making someone accept us. It was about removing the legal restrictions on living here. We won the legal right to vote in the 1950's, fought for the right to compete in the 1960's, went to school and into business in the 1970's, established our businesses in the 1980's, and have prospered ever since.

We do not need anything else except the yoke of our make-believe leaders off our backs. You see, it is the leaders who are the most threatened by a strong Black community. If we were strong, we would not need leaders. We are not a tribe, and we do not need tribal chiefs. We are a diverse community with different voices and many different customs. Some like Jazz, some like Gospel, some are Christian and some are Muslim, some are rich and some are poor. We now have the opportunity to become great in America. We owe it to the silent voices of our ancestors to thrive here. Success is the greatest revenge.

The Black community is awakening! We are beginning to see and understand the secrets of success: not looking to leaders but becoming leaders! We are depending on ourselves in spite of who may not like us. We are learning from the past while preparing for the future. The Black community must now struggle with itself. Success is ours if we want to take it. It will never be ours if we wait for someone to give it.

Do not be fooled by the old saying, *"Give a man a fish and he will eat for a day. Teach him to fish and he will eat for a lifetime."* We do not need to be taught or given anything. *"Just open the gate onto the lake, and I will need nothing else to feed myself!"*

Black Reparations and the "Forty Acres and A Mule" Syndrome Won't Work

Here we go again folks: on talk shows, call-in programs, and the print media, the old dream that wouldn't go away, reparations! "Give me my forty acres and a mule! I can't go on with my life until you have made me whole." Has anyone really taken a good long look at what Black people are asking for, and what we are saying about ourselves?

If we could prosper shortly after the Civil War achiev-

Would Black people need to pay back the government for education received under the Affirmative Action program and Head Start? Would Black people get a bill for all the job training and placement given to "low-income, disadvantaged youth" programs? If we are going to say reparations are a "payback" for all that we have suffered, then all of the other programs we received during the 1960's and 1970's need to be paid back as well. The Japanese internment victims received no special assistance except the reparation payments; therefore, we should be required to repay all of the other special benefits designed to alleviate the legacy of slavery.

There are too many variables making this far too complicated to work. Reparations are therefore a waste of time and energy. Let us get on with what works: education, competition, dedication, morality, family and faith. These are the principles that freed us and prospered us. We are presently the greatest group of Black people on this planet. This proposal simply will never happen, and if it does, it would benefit very few of us.

Black Progress In the 1980's: Those Good Old Reagan Years

Have you heard about those Reagan Years? You know, those terrible years of greed and selfishness? You remember, the decade of oppression for Black and poor people. Yes, those years we are supposed to be paying for now with higher taxes and more government control over our lives.

You have heard all the rhetoric about the 1980's, but have you seen much data?

Where is the evidence of injustice to Blacks and the poor? It seems prosperity is racist. Making a living or educating yourself is a sellout.

I have heard all of the terrible statements about the

73

decade of the 1980's. When I asked for evidence I was given long blank stares like I was from Mars. No one ever asks for the details. Why would I not simply believe my leaders? It was as if Black people were a tribe and only our tribal chiefs could speak for us. Why should I buy into this notion that the Reagan years were unprofitable for Black people? I decided I could not, at least not without the evidence, so I researched it for myself.

What I found was prosperity of unequal heights, progress as never seen in the Black community. Whatever happened to us in the 1980's, Black people need to work toward more of it. We should study this decade closely and figure out what occurred and how we can repeat it. According to a brochure issued in September 1993 by the U.S. Department of Commerce, Economics and Statistics Administration Bureau of the Census, in 1790, when the first census was taken, Black people numbered about 760,000. In 1860, at the start of the Civil War, the Black population increased to 4.4 million, but the percentage of the overall U.S. population dropped to 14 percent from 19 percent. Most were slaves, with only 488,000 counted as freemen. By 1900, our population had doubled and reached 8.8 million.

In 1910, about 90 percent of the Black population lived in the South, but large numbers began migrating north, looking for better job opportunities and living conditions. The Black population reached the 15 million mark in 1950 and was close to 27 million in 1980. In 1990 the Black population numbered about 30 million and represented 12 percent of the total population, the same proportion as in 1900. The 13% population growth between 1980 and 1990 was one-third higher than the national growth of 10%.

The Black voting-age population increased to 20.4 million in 1990 from 17.1 million in 1980. In 1990, the proportion of Black Americans 25 years old and over completing high school rose from 51% in 1980 to 63% in 1990 (see the Census Bureau statistics in the back of this book). In 1940, only 7% of Black people 25 years old and over had completed high school. Among the Black population, a slightly higher proportion of females (64%) than males (62%) had completed high school.[7] Black people became more independent, made more money, attended college in greater numbers and became homeowners in more cases than ever before.

With so much positive news, so much progress, so much to look forward to, why so little news about the progress of Black Americans in the 1990's? You would think the civil rights leaders would be shouting and calling for a national day of celebration! Here we have the first decade that Black Americans finally had begun to fulfill the dreams of so many of our ancestors. Finally, we had won the legal right to join in the American dream of pursuing happiness and dignity. After hundreds of years of praying and sacrificing, Black Americans took advantage of the 1980's and haven't looked back since.

The 1980's ushered in the greatest peacetime economic expansion this country has ever had. Jobs were plentiful and American confidence was high. Black Americans hit the 1980's with full force. Educated, motivated and dedicated, Black Americans found themselves in the greatest economic, political and social revival since the decade following the civil war.

The Census Data Points Out The Following Information On The Decade Of The 1980's
EDUCATION:
During the decade of the 1980's, from 1980 to 1990, the proportion of Black Americans 25 years old and over who completed high school rose from 51% (1980) to 63% (1990). The high school dropout rate for Black Ameri-

cans decreased from 16% to 14% in the same period. So much for the crisis mentality of our Black youth in education. We are staying in school and furthering our education. The 1990 census showed two million Black people enrolled in college. This is a 150% increase over the 1980 figure.

POVERTY:

In 1990 8.4 million Black people were considered poor. That is much too many, and the 20 million Black people who are NOT poor are still too few. The numbers are heading in the right direction, though. By 1993, approximately 70% of Black Americans were living above the poverty levels.

HOME OWNERS:

From 1980 to 1990 home ownership in the Black community increased from 3.7 million to 4.3 million. Forty-three percent of the Black population lived in homes they either owned or were buying. The median value of homes owned by Black Americans increased by 63% from 1980 to 1990.

We did not stop as the 1990's got under way. Nothing can seem to stop the progress after so many years of limited access into the American dream. Even during the economic downturn, Black businesses have thrived. Sales and employment at the nation's largest Black-owned businesses saw tremendous increases in 1993. According to an article in the Escondido, California, *Times-Advocate* newspaper, written by Rick Gladstone of the Associated Press, sales and employment at the nation's biggest Black-owned companies surged in 1993. These figures outpaced the growth rates of their White-owned counterparts. Moreover, while the biggest mainstream manufacturing and service businesses continued to slash jobs in 1993, the companies in the *Black En-*

terprise top 100 showed a 22% increase in employment. The magazine attributed the improvements to a fitful but unmistakable economic recovery, a spending boom helped by the tonic of lower interest rates, an expensive Japanese yen that made American cars more affordable and Black-owned car dealerships more profitable, and the underlying tenacity of Black entrepreneurs.

Despite fierce competition and an undependable economy, Black businesses were able to achieve greater productivity from increasingly scarce resources. Black-owned businesses yielded a record breakthrough of over $10 billion in revenue, according to Earl G. Graves, *Black Enterprise* publisher. The top Black-owned companies posted annual sales gains that tripled the percentages of Fortune 500 companies. The detractors would point out how far we have to go; I would point out how far we have come.

The *Black Enterprise* Magazine Reports How the Nation's Top Black-Owned Businesses Made Their Money In the Millions of Dollars in 1993.
Sales by Industry:

Media	**9.5%**	**$979.797**
Manufacturing	**5.4%**	**$556.006**
Construction	**3.4%**	**$345.506**
Health & Beauty Aids	**2.5%**	**$258.616**
Engineering	**1.7%**	**$179.119**
Technology	**7.8%**	**$806.278**

OTHER (Commodities, Entertainment, Health Care, Security & Maintenance, Transportation, and Miscellaneous.)
4.1%   **$415.188**

I would be the first to note the hard work ahead of us. This is not beginning to be enough. But all I hear is how impossible it is out there and how much of a disadvantage we have. We should be cautious of Black leaders who make their living providing services to the poor and representing the down and out. It might be in their best interest to keep you down and out and not in competition with them.

I now understand why so many Black leaders are running around saying they will get more services for the poor. Have you ever heard them speak about getting you out of poverty? It is time to leave the plantation and live your life.

Chapter Six

The Real Dream!

"A gentleman will not insult me, and no man not a gentleman can insult me."

Frederick Douglass

January 15th marks the birthday of Martin Luther King Jr. and the beginning of massive celebrations nationwide in remembrance and honor of Dr. King. However, I wonder, have we lost sight of his dream? Are we confusing the many messages and goals of the civil rights movement with King's dream? Was the dream of Dr. King the same dream as Malcolm X, Huey Newton or H. Rap Brown? Can today's youth properly remember Dr. King's legacy by the words of Angela Brown or Donald De Freeze "Cynque?"

When I see all of the "African American" celebrations on King's birthday, I wonder. All I see are Black people dressing in modern (not traditional) African clothing, beating drums and tying colorful cloths around their heads. It seems the focus of the celebration is centered on our African past instead of our American future.

When I see the African dance groups, the African storytellers, the African drum beaters and all of the crafts and clothing for sale during this season, I must wonder, just what was the dream? It seems like there is a strong Pan-African movement today, and every Black celebration is moving toward the African identity. If Martin Luther King Jr. were alive today, would he be wearing the African clothing and beating on a drum? Or would he be reminding us of our American roots and encouraging us to take stock in our "American" culture and become part of the American mainstream?

I went back and reread his books and speeches. It does not appear that he thought very much about his Africanism (I am not saying he was not proud of it). He focused on our Americanism. Dr. King seemed to be working under the assumption that Black Americans had every right to assume full partnership with America. We have farmed her land, built her factories, worked free for generations, and fought and died in every one of her wars. Black Americans were a very important part of building America into the greatest country on earth, and we should be assuming our position in her future.

Martin Luther King Dreamed Of A Day When All Americans Could Participate Freely In the American Dream

Dr. King's dream did not separate people into subcommunities trying to keep alive every cultural tradition from our ancestors. Dr. King seemed to be a patriot, someone who loved America, not for what it had been but for what it could be, thus the dream.

No one is trying to deny the harm of slavery, but I am trying to call attention to what slavery could not do to us: destroy our soul. Slavery forced nine generations to develop self-hatred, no respect for families, little care for education, and general hopelessness. But I choose to give more time and credibility to the success of Black Americans despite the burdens of slavery.

We Should Not Focus On the Suffering Without Honoring the Victory Over Suffering

Never, in the history of mankind, has a nation or nationality accomplished so much with so little. We should celebrate the victory instead of nagging about a need for the war. We won! Humanity won, Africa won, and America has won. The slave master lost. He thought his lifestyle would last forever and his children would also be masters.

Now our worst enemy seems to be ourselves. We are afraid to claim the victory which is right in front of us and available for all who would claim it. Freedom means responsibility! Responsibility for your own success and for your own failures. If you can blame someone else for your failures or look to others for your success, you are still a slave and dependent on the master.

It takes guts to be free! It takes the willingness to fail and the willingness to be responsible for those failures. Freedom is often a solitary journey and others may not want to travel that path. Freedom is an individual journey, not a group journey. Slavery was the group journey we experienced together. You can experience freedom—but you must decide for yourself.

Affirmative Action and the Beauty of the American Conscience—None are Free Until All are Free

We are a nation of conscience and action. More than once we have examined our treatment of one another and literally torn ourselves apart to change. We did that in the American Revolution, the Civil War and the Civil Rights Movement. America is not afraid to challenge herself and correct past mistakes. America is a nation of courageous individuals struggling to achieve harmony with the differences among us. Yes, this nation has a cruel past. However, the very nation that created such cruelty and shame also was the nation that tore itself apart to correct it.

We survived because of the conscience of America and a true dedication to the creed that "All men are created equal." We survived because most Americans realized no one could be free until all of us were free. The journey included struggling through the problems, because struggling together made our nation stronger.

The treatment of Black Americans after the Civil War could not be hidden and forgotten, nor accepted. Because it could not be ignored and would not go away, it had to be changed. However, Black people are not pet animals in need of America's care and protection. Without the ability to compete, Black Americans will wither and die.

The well-meaning proponents of affirmative action only want to help us. They feel our pain and want us to get better. I suspect the real motivation is to alleviate their own feelings of guilt and shame. Because of the self-esteem problems their ancestors have left them with, Black Americans have been placed into the same category of "save the whales, rain forest and spotted owl," to be studied, adored, respected and protected. We have become the special cause of many groups, and to some, we are the "White man's burden."

We have achieved more in this country than anywhere else on the planet because of competition—not compassion, sympathy, caring, or feelings. We want to compete with White America. We demand a right to take all we can earn. We will not be satisfied with a share of the pie that the leftists set aside for us. We can earn more than your allowance. Keep the set-aside programs and quotas; they only keep us from competing for the whole pie.

Most Americans Understand What Success Is

Success grows out of the problems you go through, not the problems you go around. Affirmative action allows us to avoid the problems and keeps us from growing. Could it be that the patronizing, sympathetic rhetoric of the left only disguises their true intentions: keeping Black

Americans from competing and winning against them and their children?

James L. Robinson sent chills over the civil rights leaders with his book *Racism or Attitude,* where he gave notice that Black Americans would no longer blame White America for the troubles in our community. Robinson says: *"The great challenge facing Black Americans today is the task of taking control of their own future by exerting the necessary leadership, making the required sacrifices, and building the needed institutions so that Black social and economic development becomes a reality."*

Affirmative action allows liberals to feel like they are doing something important. It makes the Black recipients doubtful, resentful, angry and unfulfilled. Your expectations become your "entitlements" instead of your potential. Ambition, which takes action, turns into "set-asides," which take waiting. We know the game and we do not want to play anymore. All of the leftist liberals and their self-appointed Black tribal chiefs need to understand we will never go back onto the plantation. We will never again allow them to dictate, regulate, instigate, and humiliate us with "good deeds." We will compete with them so that what we gain will be ours on merit alone.

We Have Begun To Look At the Results of Affirmative Action and Not Listen To the Stated Intentions

Based upon that analysis, we reject affirmative action as divisive and harmful. Let us outlaw discrimination based on race. Let us make hiring practices based upon the color of our skin against the law. That would affirm our national dream of colorblindness and reflect the right kind of action.

I appreciate and understand the kindness and compassion of those who want to "help." However, I do not find compassion in the old saying: *"If you give a man a fish, he'll eat for a day. If you teach him to fish, he will eat for a lifetime."* I understand your love, but please understand my frustration. You do not need to "give" me anything. This is suggesting that you have it and I do not. It is suggesting that you are superior to me, and I cannot survive without your compassion. I do not believe you intended to give me these feelings, and I hold no grudge against you. In addition, may I also suggest that you do not have to teach me how to fish? Again it gives you a superior position over me and is not good for my self-esteem to believe it. I have a better saying for you (it is a "Masonism"): *"Just open the gate and let me on to the lake. I'll need nothing else to feed myself."* I need you to get out of my way so I can launch my own boat and feed my family and myself. Thanks-- and I will see you at sea.

Affirmative action was a good moral experiment, but it has failed and must be replaced by fair competition. Competition makes everyone stronger and that is good for the country. We are able to compete, and we can win. Lower the barriers, remove the artificial obstacles, and let the games begin.

Jesse Jackson Has Lost Sight

On November 2, 1983, President Reagan signed a bill into law that designated the third Monday of January as a Federal holiday in honor of Dr. Martin Luther King. The next day Jesse Jackson declared he was running for Reagan's job! I had long before decided Jesse would never be satisfied. I had grown tired of waiting for the civil rights leaders to stop whining and begin to celebrate the victory. I knew there were still problems in America, but could we not find something that could lift our spirits?

No there was always a problem, always a crisis, always victims, never victorious. Jesse Jackson was running for president only to demonstrate to the Democratic Party how many Black American voters stood behind him. His value as an activist was predicated on the number of the tribe he could deliver to the master on Election Day.

The overseers no longer had to worry about keeping the slaves in the field picking cotton. The new slaves were no longer picking cotton; they were just having their votes picked by one political party.

It had finally dawned on me, as a young Berkeley student, that Democrats really understood poverty and poor people. In my studies, I began to think and rationalize. After decades of the war on poverty, some things were clear, at least to the Democrats. It is worth repeating: they knew that if you place poor people in one area together it is guaranteed to do certain things. It is guaranteed to breed teen pregnancies, drug usage, bad schools, low self-esteem, high taxes and unemployment. They also know it is guaranteed to breed "Democratic voters."

They have found out that the poorer the community, the more its members are dependent on Democrats for services and the more they will vote for them. You will never find a poor, economically ravaged community voting for Republicans. It is in the best interest of Democrats to have as many poor and dependent people as possible. Every program they want will always isolate the poor from the rich and provide services for the poor, but never provide services to get you un-poor.

However, the people may be beginning to wake up. No longer are we blindly following our self-anointed leaders. Their crowds are smaller and their effectiveness is weakening. Except for the media that love these whining, negative social leaches, most Americans are not paying much attention.

Instead of leadership, we have gotten the plantation mentality. Just look at the controversy over "Ebonics."

"The Ebonic Plague"

A group called the "Task Force on the Education of African-American Students" claims many Black students should be classified as bilingual because they speak an inner-city dialect. Whether one calls it Black English, Ebonics, Slang or Ghettoeze, it is not a different language but a handicap. Do they not know their history; do they not know why Black children speak in broken English?

When Africans arrived here, they had to be "broken." Being "broken" meant having your heritage, culture and dignity literally beaten out of you. The slaves were not allowed to speak any language except the master's language. The Slave Breakers taught the Africans just enough English to allow them to follow instructions. They could not pronounce their words properly for fear of the whip.

The Slave Breakers understood that education and communication would increase the opportunity of independence. They did not want a population of Africans reading the Declaration of Independence or the Federalist Papers. They wanted Black people who could follow simple instructions and get back to work. Their worst fear was a clear-thinking Black population contemplating equality.

There were laws against speaking proper English or learning to read and write. Frederick Douglass, Denmark Vessey, Harriet Tubman and Toussant L'Overture taught themselves enough to desire freedom, and that was the fear of the Slave Breaker. Today the Black community is still under the fear and influence of the Slave Driver. These new slave drivers are saying we should be proud of the broken language master's whips have given us.

Black English has no social benefits for anyone; it prepares you for failure and victimization. If the Oakland Board of Education members had any interest in the future of their children, they would reject the recommendations of this task force. Then they would embark upon a crash program to encourage English and discourage the use of slang.

I cannot help noticing that all of the civil rights leaders have mastered the English language. Louis Farrakhan, Jesse Jackson, Dr. Martin Luther King, Malcolm X, Stokely, Newton, H. Rap Brown, all had a mastery of the language. Even ex-slaves like Crispus Attucks, Frederick Douglass and Booker T. Washington had complete mastery of our language. They knew that education was freedom, and the slave master knew broken English was slavery; why did the task force not know this?

However, let us get to the real reason for this task force. Black English is not new. I recently wrote about Amherst College offering a course in it. I remember colleges offering studies in this and other slang languages while I was a student. Is it just an excuse for poor verbal skills in the Black community? Is it part of some conspiracy to keep the Black man down? No, it is simply about money and power and who will control it.

Recently, millions of Federal Bilingual Education dollars were riding on the Ebonics debate. If Oakland could convince the Federal government that Black American children should be in a bilingual program, local school districts would have been in line for more Federal dollars. Black children would have spent the school day studying the root meaning of "Cool," "What up," and "Kick'n it," while their White counterparts were studying college prep English courses. Maybe the task force was depending on "Affirmative Action" to allow these Black children into college anyway.

It is shameful that these so-called educators were willing to sell the future of these children just to receive more Federal money. There is one often-used word still with us from slavery, a word that is often used in the Black community. This word described a traitor against the plot to escape the plantation. This word was reserved for the Black person who traded the plans to the master for a scrap of food. For a little blood money the community was sold out. It was called being a "sellout."

This Oakland School Board of Education and "Ebonics" dominated the talk show topics, news reports and general conversations among the population. We seemed motivated to assure each other of our mutual agreement that this was a silly, weak excuse for failure.

The Oakland school board really opened our eyes to the failure of government education. These professional bureaucrats spent millions of tax dollars, tried numerous programs and still failed to teach the very basics in education. They have come before us and have admitted failure; they have recognized that the children under their care cannot read, write or speak the native tongue of this nation.

After taking our money and failing, what did they do? They asked for more money to teach teachers. Teachers already know how to read, write and speak the language. These educators expected us to pay for a weekend getaway conference so teachers could study "Ebonics."

They tell us the Black children speak a different dialect and cannot understand the instructions given by teachers. This is strange since these same children can understand television programs and music. They can read comic books and the sports page but not textbooks. They can learn the lyrics of the latest song the day it is released, and some can tell you everything that happened on the television soap operas.

Nevertheless, we must be sensitive and understanding. One should not criticize the Oakland School District; after all, they are the professionals. Education! Do not try this at home, folks; leave it to the professionals. I will not mention the church schools in those same neighborhoods that are teaching English successfully. It would be too mean to draw your attention to the private schools and home schools that are working in the community. Therefore, I will not give in to the temptation.

Because of the new kinder and gentler Mason Weaver, I will ask for the expansion of Ebonics in concept. After all, if Ebonics will work for Black children speaking Slang, it would work for other cultures in our community. I have been e-mailed some of your suggestions for Ebonics-style learning for other ethnic and social groups.

In the spirit of diversity, tolerance and unity, let me share some of the better ones with you. Coming soon to a government school near you, Ebonics multiplied.

1. Irish-American—Leprechaunics
2. Native-American—Kimosabics
3. Chinese-American—Won-tonics
4. Japanese-American—Mama-san-ics
5. Jewish-American—Zionics
6. Eskimo-American—Harpoonics
7. German-American—Autobahnics
8. French-American—Escargonics
9. Danish-American—Pastryonics
10. Red Neck-American—Bubonics
11. Washington-American—Taxonics
12. Oakland School Board—Moronics

Sounds foolish, right? No matter who you are, it is equally insulting, demeaning and condescending to you. So is Ebonics to Black people. The discussion should have been concerned with the merits of this proposal. We should have planned for the immediate recall of this un-qualified school board. This was not only insulting, it was child abuse!

The "Ebonic Plague" is already a full epidemic! When school administrators in Oakland, California, proposed teaching "Ebonics" as a second language, many of you did not know that "Black English" was already part of the education program. Many of our children have been subjected to the abusive and dangerous notion that skin color, race and culture have a language of their own. The fight over "Ebonics" (or Ghettoeze as I prefer) is not about preventing its start, but to stop the existing program.

Since 1981 the California State Department of Education has carried out a program called "Proficiency in Standard English for Speakers of Black Language." This program distributes Ebonics staff development and lesson plan materials to school districts. The material explicitly directs teachers to incorporate something called "Black Language" into the class work. It also decides that "Black Language" is an appropriate alternative to correct English in some situations.

I have received the official Lesson Plan Handbook for the program and it is sad. The plan tells the teachers to "Kill these myths." The following is what the lesson plan calls "myths:"

1. Standard English is the correct way to speak at all times.
2. Standard English is "White English."
3. Poor people do not communicate as well as profes sional people.

Do you believe these are myths? Standard English is English; everything else is slang. There is no "home language" and "school language," but these professionals think so. Slang should never be considered appropriate by educators. We should encourage our children to speak English in class and on the playground.

The lesson plan does the opposite. It encourages slang in some situations. The plan has teachers brainstorming with children to think up situations in which "school language" should be used and when something called "playground language" would be better. This State of California's plan actually requires Black children to be taught the use of "Playground language" when talking to their "good friends" and "playing with their brother."

The proper use of language is to use it properly, always. The more you use it outside the classroom the more proficient you will be. From 1973 to 1975, I studied Swahili as a second language. The Swahili students used the language during lunch, social events, parties and whenever we came into contact with each other. New students in the program and older students always spoke Swahili to each other whenever social contact was made. The out-of-school use of this language is the reason I still speak Swahili today, twenty-plus years later. If I spoke Swahili only in class, and only English on the playground, I would speak only English today. These educators do not seem to know this, and that is why they are so dangerous to our children.

There was an intelligent response to the Ebonics insanity. California State Senator Ray Haynes introduced Senate Bill 205, which would have prohibited the use of state taxpayer dollars to fund Ebonics education programs. This bill would have eliminated the State Department of Education's "Proficiency in Standard English for Speakers of Black Language" program. It would have preempted school districts from applying for Federal bilingual funding for Ebonics programs. Senator Haynes' bill failed to make it out of the committee, due to the efforts of a Black State Senator named Diane Watson. In spite of Senate hearings and testimonies of myself and others, Senator Watson acted to guard the slave masters' house while the slaves toiled in the fields. Again, we have proven to be our worst enemy. If a White politician had suggested Ebonics, there would have been rioting in the streets.

Senator Haynes is inspired by President Kennedy, who once said: "A child miseducated is a child lost." This is a very courageous move on Senator Haynes' part. The argument over "Ebonics" is presented as a "Black issue" but Senator Haynes correctly sees it as a California issue. Senator Haynes has said, "Ebonics education has fast become a statewide concern because, if implemented, it has the potential to miseducate an entire generation of children by lowering academic standards and legitimizing incorrect English."

SB 205 and existing law require English as the basic language of instruction in all public schools. This bill, known as the "Equality in English Instruction Act," recognizes that English is the language of success, business and politics. Senator Haynes' bill may be California's best inoculation against the "Ebonic Plague."

However, what does history have to say about education of Black people? What would the ancestors from slavery days think of this proposal? Let us look at the words of one of the great orators of our day. Frederick Douglass fought slavery and mistreatment by way of education. In an era where teaching a slave to read or write was against the law, he saw it as a ticket to freedom. Here is an excerpt from his own narrative of his life. He speaks about education and the system that benefits from your not having it.

Frederick Douglass, an escaped slave, gives us the best response to Ebonics from his writings.

Frederick Douglass in his NARRATIVE

Very soon after I went to live with Mr. and Mrs. Auld, she very kindly commenced to teach me the A, B, C. After I had learned this, she assisted me in learning to spell words of three or four letters. Just at this point of my progress, Mr. Auld found out what was going on, and at

once forbade Mrs. Auld to instruct me further, telling her, among other things, that it was unlawful, as well as unsafe, to teach a slave to read. To use his own words, further, he said, " If you give a nigger an inch, he will take an ell. A nigger should know nothing but to obey his master to do as he is told to do. Learning would spoil the best nigger in the world. Now," said he, "if you teach that nigger (speaking of myself) how to read, there would be no keeping him. It would forever fit him to be a slave. He would at once become unmanageable, and of no value to his master. As to himself it could do him no good, but a great deal of harm. It would make him discontented and unhappy." These words sank deep into my heart, stirred up sentiments within that lay slumbering, and called into existence an entirely new train of thought. It was a new and specialized revolution, explaining dark and mysterious things, with which my youthful understanding had struggled, but struggled in vain. I now understood what had been to me a most perplexing difficulty — to whit, the White man's power to enslave Black men. It was a grand achievement, and I prized it highly. From that moment, I understood the pathway from slavery to freedom. (Frederick Douglass, *Narrative of the Life of Frederick Douglass, An American Slave. Written by himself*) Edited by Benjamin Quarles. Pages 58-59.

All over the South it was against the law for Black people (free or slave) to be educated. There was a serious effort to keep reading and writing out of the hands of Black people.

In April of 1812 it was reported that Savannah, Georgia, had enacted a city ordinance that called for a $30 fine for any person who "teaches any person of colour, slave or free, to read or write." So not only were slaves forbidden to read or write, so were free Black Americans. The notion of Black people reading or writing or even speaking proper English was considered useless.

South Carolina in 1749 (while still only a province) enacted this law: "Whereas the having of slaves taught to write, or suffering them to be employed in writing, may be attended with great inconveniences, Be it enacted, That all and every person and persons whatsoever, who shall hereafter teach or cause any slave to be taught to write, or shall use or employ any slave as a scribe in any manner of writing whatsoever hereafter taught to write, every such person or persons shall, for every such offence, forfeit the sum of one hundred pounds current money." It was against the law to hire an educated Black person.

Virginia's code of 1819 enforced that "any school or schools for teaching them reading or writing either in the day or night would be considered an unlawful assembly." (Sketch of the Laws relating to Slavery in the several states of the United States of America by George M. Stroud, 1837.)

All over the South, dusty law books give testimony of the real history of "Ebonics" and the Oakland School District's goals, real or imagined. The old Southern slave states knew Black people could learn to read and write. If Ebonics was natural to Black people, we would not find so many laws against teaching Black people to read or write. What the slave master understood, the school board members still don't get: EDUCATION IS FREEDOM!

Poor education is now a national disgrace and it covers all races and classes. We are allowing our schools to graduate children unprepared for the world, and that is child abuse. Even our colleges are bending under the onslaught of high tuition and lower-achieving students from the nation's high schools.

A recent survey points to the ever-increasing cost of college education. The top schools can cost close to $30,000 a year just for tuition and supplies. When you add the cost of room and board, transportation and other costs, the investment in a college degree is very high. I could discuss the real reasons costs are increasing, but we do not have the space. I will not discuss the tuition price-fixing or the cost for professors who do not teach, and we will leave for another day the lack of quality instructors in our colleges.

What amazes me are the classes offered and the social engineering we are asked to pay for. When you send your child to college, the minimal expectation is their preparation to earn a living and compete in society. However, a review of courses offered at some of the most prestigious universities of our nation reveals an astonishing collection of useless classes aimed at indoctrination, not education.

While parents are saving and sacrificing to pay for college education, the colleges are offering classes in "Lesbian Novels Since World War II," "Queering the Renaissance" and "Witches, Saints, and Seers." Classes are offered as socially enlightening but in reality serve to desensitize us to racism, homosexual lifestyles, witchcraft, anti-Americanism, and radical environmentalism.

At the University of California, San Diego, class number 156 of the Ethnic Studies Department was titled "Civil Liberties —The Rights of Criminals and Minorities." It examined the rights of "marginal" groups such as aliens, illegal immigrants, and the mentally ill, all in the context of discrimination. All of us should know our rights, but this class focused on America as discriminating against the criminals and mentally ill. Other interesting classes offered were Political Science 107a, "Gay and Lesbian Politics," and the ever-popular Sociology 170, "Sociology of Fashion."

A look over the course description of UC Santa Cruz's American Studies 175, "Generation X," shows some confusion about what the class offered. "Twentysomethings? Baby busters? Slackers? Whiners? Who/what/when/where/why is 'GenerationX'—and who cares anyway? Traditional or progressive? Wealthy or wannabe? White or Colorful? Multicultural or uncultured? Repressive or oversexed? Spiritual or technological? Courageous, apathetic, or terrified?" Did they leave anyone out? What is more frightening than the empty-headed classes that will lead to no future employment skills is that we pay for them.

While classes are overcrowded, tuition is rising and college stays are longer, why fill the catalog with classes like "Black Marxism" (UC Santa Barbara), "Imaginary Women" (UCLA) or "Inequality and Social Class" (UC Riverside)? With cuts in research, business schools and equipment, why are we paying the professors to teach such feel-good classes? These courses may be of interest, but the university-level education is not where to find it. Maybe these professors should be at a junior college night school.

The problem is not limited to California schools or public schools. Across the nation, we have an onslaught of social engineering classes designed to give a certain political or social point of view. At Harvard, you have a class on "Fetishism," Princeton has "Income Distribution," and Yale offers "The United Nations, Statecraft, and the Search for a New World Order."

Who would think Amherst College would offer a course on "Black English?" Instead of encouraging Black Americans to speak the language of success, business and politics (English), we now have our own language to claim.

Isn't multiculturalism great? These classes are usually considered easy courses resulting in high grades, so many students take them as electives. The professors grade easy to attract the students, but the parents lose because no educating is going on. These courses are great for the grade-point average but a poor excuse for higher education. Poor education cannot serve society except those who wish to control it.

As president of The Committee to Restore America, I traveled to San Francisco for the University of California regents meeting on July 20, 1995. They were gathered to vote on Regent Ward Connerly's proposal to ban racial preferences in hiring and admissions within the U.C. system. It was as if I had never left the 1960's with so many of the same groups doing the same things as before. When I was a radical militant student at U.C. Berkeley, I considered many of these groups my allies. We were demanding equal rights and equal opportunity. We demanded the elimination of race as a criterion for hiring. We fought against discrimination because it was wrong.

However, something was different about the groups that gathered in protest that morning. They were joined by a strange alliance. Other groups like the Socialist Workers Party, the Communist Party and many other openly anti-American groups had prominent positions. I began to think, "What was the real goal of the 1960's? Did we fight to destroy America, or for inclusion 'in' America?" We were there in force and we were there to speak out against racial policies that allowed for discrimination of one race over another. These principles are what I fought and struggled for in the 1960's and 1970's.

As we observed the planned demonstrations and organized media events, I soon began to notice other groups like ours. Hundreds of students and citizens were standing together demanding an end to racism and discrimination. Despite the news reports and sound bites, despite the organized attempts to fill the campus with revolutionaries, despite giving attention and importance to groups because they made the most noise, truth prevailed.

America showed up that morning of July 20, 1995, and you would have been proud of her. I believe most of the students came to support the proposal of Ward Connerly. They were not the loudest, they were not marching and they did not try to disrupt the meeting, but they were there to be counted. The fact that distracters could not close down the meeting was due to lack of support rather than overwhelming police presence. As a matter of fact, when Jesse Jackson finally led his march of protest, he had very few people with him, so few that the regents were still able to vote without much disruption, and the police simply ignored them until they grew weary and went home.

It was a great day for the civil rights movement. It was a great day for America. It was the best evidence to date that the civil rights movement has been won and the battle over legal exclusion is over. The July 20, 1995, meeting was a victory celebration and a confirmation of the goals of the civil rights movement. It was a declaration that the war has been won and we are beginning to build up America. We are not allowing ourselves to be separated into racial groups.

Despite the efforts of a dozen or so activists inside the meeting and a few hundred bused-in groups standing outside, America won. We are a country of conscience and a country of freedom. We have often fallen short in our past and have many more battles to overcome. However, America has regained her conscience. It was very encouraging to witness people, who had previously been openly and legally discriminated against, stand up for the rights of their past oppressors. Truth is not relative—it is absolute. It is not directed by our will but directs the will of honest people. The truth has determined that discrimination based upon the color of one's skin or gender is wrong for every group and should not be tolerated by any group.

Now we must move to address the real problems and prepare ourselves to compete. Some groups are not competing in the marketplace as well as others. The solution cannot be to discriminate against the achieving group. The solution should be to identify and rectify the problems within the underachieving group. We can do that both as a nation and as a community. Yes, racism is still among us, prejudice still raises its ugly head, and some people still consider one gender less capable than the other. However, we have broken the back of Jim Crow, and the false images and stereotypes are falling fast.

It was great to visit the Bay area again. It was heartwarming to see so many of my old comrades in the struggle stand up for America. It was nice to hear them say, "We have won." Now comes the hard part: the peace. In order to have peace, we must be willing to depart from some past allies and join some past adversaries. However, the same American spirit that won the battle can win the peace!

Civil Rights Groups Have No Shame

The battle over affirmative action is really heating up. All of the social groups that cater to "victims" finally have an issue for which they can rally the troops. The anger and distortions have only begun as they try to separate and alienate us from each other. Before the issue of affirmative action arrived we could only guess at their true motivations. We were just confused; they would claim to be for the people but then advocate programs that only hurt and redirected progress.

Like the Black leaders, these social groups receive their

power and influence by providing services for the poor. They get funding and status by keeping the disadvantaged dependent upon them. Therefore, they have no real interest in resolving the problems of our society, only exploiting them.

Take Jesse Jackson, a man desperately in need of an issue. He visited California often in 1995-96 to protest the affirmative action progress we had made. Even the press ignored him and they are his meal ticket. So what did he do? He decided to protest and demonstrate at the U.C. Board of Regents meeting in San Francisco on July 20th. Though he had been invited publicly to participate, he declared that he would disrupt the proceedings and risk arrest. He claimed he would "lay his body on the line" to keep "us" from going back thirty years. Even at his planned civil disobedience, the fifty ministers who he promised were ready to go to jail turned out to be closer to five. The demonstration was so small that when they blocked an intersection to force their arrest, they were just ignored.

The real problem is that Jesse Jackson has made a lot of money on poverty and misery. He reminds me of the tribal chiefs who sold Black people into slavery for a few trinkets and gifts. I firmly believe that Jesse Jackson understands what real progress is and how to achieve it. He has done well and so have his children. They do not wait for government set-asides and special programs. His family members are self-motivated, have become educated and are all achieving their goals here in America.

Nevertheless, according to Jackson, that is not good enough for you and me. We must continue to depend on the group to lead us. We must continue to follow the tribal chiefs who dictate to us. If we set out on our own we are called names like "Oreo," "Uncle Tom" and so on.

Jesse Jackson demonstrated in San Francisco because his income was at stake. He must reenergize the hopelessness in the Black community so they will look to him as their savior. Jesse Jackson will continue to fight real progress in the Black community, because real progress reduces the need for leaders—and Jesse Jackson makes his living being a leader.

I hope the Black community will not fall for this insult to our intelligence. However, unless there is a special government program with government administrators looking over them, some groups will continue to fight against us. Real freedom means independence—not co-dependence.

The Black community is fully capable of standing on its own two feet. We have never needed Big Brother, Uncle Sam, or benevolent liberal Democrats to "ride cover" for us.

Jesse Jackson is not alone. All of the old-time civil rights groups have joined the battle for the same reasons: because they need an issue. The Black community rejected their whining and scare tactics long ago. The NAACP had financial problems because of a drop in membership, not corporate sponsorships. They have been out of step with the Black community for some time and we have not followed them. The press has followed them and reflected their dogma as that of the Black community. The same is true of the Urban League and the Congressional Black Caucus. They all need hate and anger to survive. They all depend on non-thinking followers who depend on their leadership. This is why they have raped the community with outcome-based education and poverty programs that lead to more poverty. This is why they favor programs that force fathers out of the family and drugs into the neighborhood. This is why they want midnight basketball and not midnight libraries.

If the NAACP, Urban League, Operation PUSH and Congressional Black (African American) Caucus want a real issue they can sink their teeth into, I have a few suggestions.

Take on the welfare system that is destroying our people, or the public school system that has had disastrous results on our children. Join us, the real community, and speak on the positive elements of Black people instead of crying about how weak we are and how much we are in need. I call upon these groups to recognize that they have been used like social pimps to abuse the community and it is time to stop. I know you may lose a lot of power and influence in high places, but you will gain the respect of your people.

The Day of Atonement Began Long Ago

The "Day of Atonement" or the "Million Man March" was supposedly the reconciliation event of the Black man to his family and community. They are great slogans and inspiring goals for those easily led by emotions, but why do responsible men need to hold a public demonstration proclaiming dedication to their families? Are we to believe that Black men have just discovered family, community and responsibility?

Let us be honest—this event was simply the media's coronation of Louis Farrakhan as tribal chief of the "Black nation." This event continued the separation of the American culture to one of many nations within a nation. Now we have the homosexuals, poor, Black Americans, Mexicans, AIDS patients and women all proclaiming to be victims.

I watched much of the activities in Washington. Even if I could accept the spiritual conflict of a Muslim leading Christians, I could not overcome the vast contradictions in what was said. The mixture of atonement with blame and threats to White people and Black Americans who do not agree with the tribal chiefs seemed insincere. The call for leadership from embezzlers, unrepentant womanizers and out-of-touch socialists could not be taken seriously.

History may record 1996 as the year of "assigned leaders." Here in California, Democrat Assemblyman Willie Brown attempted to assign the Republican Speaker of the Assembly. Someone seemed bent on assigning Colin Powell as the Republican nominee for President. And now the head of a relatively small organization has been elevated to prominence and crowned leader of a whole race of people. There are probably over 20 million Black Christians in this country even if you deduct the thousands of renegades who follow Farrakhan. Why would the media consider the few thousand Black Muslims as a viable voice in our community? Why the attempt to direct and assign the role of "speaker to the Black people?"

I have been asking myself if there is anywhere else we could look for true leadership in our community. I have found many organizations that have been practicing peace, love and responsibility for years. However, because they are not angry, violent or threatening, they are not "news." Maybe if they felt more like victims and believed in massive conspiracies they could get more coverage. On the other hand, if their leaders called for separation, intimidation or reparations from White America, they would be news.

Nevertheless, these groups, individuals and organizations are simply going about their jobs of building up the community—and it is working. They saw the success in motivating people to change their lifestyles, and their success was a threat to some. Now the nationalist leadership has taken the spotlight away from the real success stories and turned over the vision to fallen rejected philosophies and groups. Again, we are led into slavery by our chiefs.

Do not blindly follow the leader. The path to true righteousness is narrow and less traveled. True community spirit stems from faith and hope, not faithlessness and hopelessness. I salute the organizations and groups that have been toiling for years in our communities. These groups have had little recognition but also tremendous success.

1. **Jesse Peterson and B.O.N.D. (Brotherhood Of New Destiny)** have represented thousands of young urban Black males determined to rebuild their lives and revitalize their neighborhood. From California and across the nation, B.O.N.D. has given hope and alternatives to helplessness.

2. **The Institute For Responsible Fatherhood and Family Revitalization**. In Cleveland, Ohio, in 1982, this organization was founded to bring young men back to the families they had created. They believe that a young man dedicated to protecting his own children will not participate in gang activity in the community. Their program discovered that once men had taken responsibility for parenthood they began to work, go to school and marry the mothers of their children. They have received a $1.5 million grant to expand their program to other cities, including San Diego.

3. **Bishop McKinney's "Block Busters"** are dedicated Christian men who meet at St. Stephen's church in San Diego, California, for prayer. They then go out and witness to gang members, drug dealers and prostitutes. They are an all-male group that is doing a very dangerous job in spite of the odds.

Then there are the nonracial groups that provide directions for community harmony on cultural bases, not ethnic considerations.

4. **"Breaking Down the Walls"** began in Oceanside, California, in 1995 to bring Christians to repentance and confessions of racial divisiveness. Four thousand people met at the Oceanside band shell that year to show love for fellow citizens. Recently this multi-racial group received

a citizenship award from the N.A.A.C.P. for its efforts.

5. **"Promise Keepers," founded by University of Colorado football coach Bill McCartney,** assembles hundreds of thousands of men each year. They proclaim seven principles to responsible manhood and community living.

All these organizations and the thousands like them are working for peace in action, not a piece of the action. They labor without recognition while we pay attention to those who make the noise. While we spend our emotions, let us remember, that sometimes the squeaky wheel does not need oil, it may need replacing.

The Return Of the American Spirit

As the century closed, I reflected upon the struggles and battles in which we have been engaged. As a community, nation and culture, we were in the midst of tremendous social and spiritual debates. We were beginning to challenge ourselves as a people and that can only be healthy. No longer were we leaving it up to so-called experts to dictate the direction our society was to go.

Our nation is beginning to distinguish between intentions and results. For far too long we have allowed educators, politicians and social leaders to take control with good ideas and great intentions. Even when the results have been disastrous, we continue to allow their leadership and directions because they are the "experts."

We continue to allow experts to tell us condom use is a healthy and effective way to discourage teen pregnancies and sexual disease, even when the evidence shows that the more you instruct "safe sex" the more dangerous and irresponsible the teenager acts. Nevertheless, with the overwhelming evidence that condoms in the hands of children are dangerous, our "experts" continue to push them.

In California, we have taken the educational system from 1st in reading to 50th in just eight years and the "experts" still want to give us more of the same. They have come into our community with smiling faces and college degrees explaining how they will help us. The result has been children who are poorly educated and less prepared to compete. Education is far too important an issue to leave up to experts. Our forefathers learned to read and write by candlelight when it was illegal to do so. Why can we not learn in these great schools? It is not possible to destroy the educational system this way by accident; it must be by design.

Once again, we have been following the tribal chiefs who make their money and gain power from the community. The spirit of those same Black power brokers who sold us to the slave masters are now delivering us to the new masters of poverty. Every family must be in control of educating its own children. Do not surrender your parental responsibility to child-abusing systems that turn out gang members.

What can we expect from a system that tells children to "Just say NO, but if you can't, here is a clean needle?" And now they are telling our children to keep marriage for later, yet still give them condoms. It's no wonder that our children have no respect for us; we are sending them mixed messages.

Then there is our government school system that has been enthusiastically following educational techniques that are total failures. Instead of correcting what the evidence shows is ineffective, they blame the failures on not enough money or the lack of parental involvement. School grades are dropping, kids have lower self-esteem, parents are burdened with high taxes and teachers are striking for more money. With the new attempt of government to dictate the careers of children and eliminate standards and grades

(School to Work programs), the citizens are finally waking up. The system will not educate, but indoctrinate our nation's children.

For more than 220 years this country has tried to live up to the creed and principles laid out in our Declaration of Independence and Constitution. We have not always reached those goals, but we have always been seeking them. We celebrate the love, sacrifices and gifts of our forebears and reflect on what we will leave our children. America must constantly reexamine herself and redirect her efforts to the ideas of freedom and personal responsibility.

It seems every problem that faces us today has a government solution, not an individual one. We are accustomed to looking to the government to resolve every need and attend to every problem we have. Instead of being independent, we have become co-dependent. Today there are no activities that do not have a government hand in them. In the land of the free and the home of the brave, we can do nothing without a government regulation, license or permission. Think of one activity or one action you can perform without government regulation or input. Try to think of one thing you have done, since you woke up this morning, which does not involve a government fee, tax, assessment, regulation or authority.

You would think that citizens of a nation that prides itself on individual freedoms could have many things that they freely enjoy. I have been looking hard for that free activity; perhaps you can help me find it. I cannot think of one thing we do that is free from our big brother in government. If you can, please write me and let me know what you find.

I thought death was free until Bill Clinton added back taxes to people who had died before he was elected. Then someone mentioned reading the Bible was free, but that would depend on where you read it and if someone was offended. How about swimming in the ocean? That must be free of government regulations. It is free except in a surfing zone, or when the beach is closed, or someone else has a conditional use permit.

The Constitution guarantees *someone* the right to keep and bear arms with no infringement. Who is that person? You have protection from having your property seized, unless you are suspected of certain illegal activities or some obscure animal wants to reside with you.

We cannot drive our cars without seat belts and speed limits and cannot repair our homes without permits. We would never consider going to a store or restaurant that did not have the proper government stamp of approval. I know we need some government protection and oversight, but do we need to be totally watched over?

Are we children and the government our parent? Oh, that reminds me, we cannot even raise our children because the government is now the parent and knows what is best. On the job, government tells private employers what salary they can pay workers. Government will dictate insurance, vacation, hiring and firing in private companies. Then the President tried to direct the way businesses handle overtime, pregnancy leave and workers' health benefits.

I would have never imagined a nation that prides itself on freedom becoming so dependent on its government. Why? What happened to the can-do spirit? We need a renewal of the property rights, individual responsibility and pride that brought us to where we are. As we remember the celebrations, picnics and fireworks of the July 4th weekend, let us also remember the reason. By self-sacrifice and dedication to principles, our nation stood up to every threat to its freedom.

What we need is a return to the spirit that made this country great. We need the spirit that allowed our prosperity and growth. We need the spirit of 1776. They dreamed of liberty from an overbearing government, not a nightmare of having an overbearing government.

This idea of Black patriotism seemed to have struck a nerve with some. Judging by my mail, calls to the radio program and e-mail, some readers believe a Black man should not long for a return to the "spirit of 1776" here and now! Some have pointed out the plight of Black people in the America of 1776. It has been suggested that I would be a helpless slave during that period.

Of course the America of 1776 had many problems, but is there a difference between the spirit and the condition of a nation or a time? The conditions of 1776 were harsh on Black people as well as poor White people. The social condition of America was not satisfactory; however, that was not the spirit. I am fully aware that Thomas Jefferson and the framers of the Declaration of Independence were speaking only of White male property owners. They excluded poor Whites, women, Indians and slaves in their dream of a free society.

However, the spirit of 1776 was much different from the condition of the times. Even during the discussions of the Declaration of Independence, the subject of slavery was a common topic. It was clear to many that a nation cannot truly be free until all of her citizens were free. It is my opinion that spirit of freedom for White male property owners spawned the eventual call for freedom of all. It was the principles laid out in those days that rallied the abolitionists, woman's suffrage and the civil rights leaders to follow.

A nation may never live up to the spirit or principles it has adopted, but great nations always try. It appears those Black people living during that period understood the call for liberty. A look at history would discover many freed and enslaved Black Americans willing to die for the liberty of White landowners. Why? Could it be that they knew what would follow? If the "spirit" of freedom takes over a land, freedom itself will follow.

That is why Crispus Attucks willingly led the citizens on that demonstration now known as the Boston Massacre. This escaped slave, living in a land that did not appreciate him as human, stepped to the front of the crowd that day. He had lived under slavery and freedom and was willing to die for freedom, even the freedom of someone else. Crispus Attucks became the first casualty of the American Revolution, the first to die for the birth of a new country. It was not for his country he died. Attucks gave his life for the call of freedom. The condition of America was hostile to him, but the spirit of freedom was worth his life to him. He died for the spirit of liberty and so did many slaves and freed Black people after him during that conflict and in every war America fought.

My family, the Weaver family, still owns property in Starksville, Mississippi. The family cemetery is there, with the graves of Weavers dating from before the Civil War. The property has been traced back to the Weaver family of 1829. Black people owning large amounts of land in Mississippi during slavery? Would Mississippi, the cruelest slave state, allow a Black family to prosper? Yes, in the midst of cruelty and death, the spirit of freedom still survived.

I do not know if I would be a slave or free in 1776. I would not want the conditions of that era to return for Black people or White. However, the Spirit of 1776 spread freedom all over the world. From the slave revolt of Haiti to the French Revolution, the spirit of 1776 was a call for freedom of freedom-loving people. Yes, we could use that spirit again today.

The 1990's Were Great for America

We have seen the sleeping giants of values, patriotism, and competition finally stir. America has been at war for the last 40 years and has not known it. Our institutions have been bombed and invaded and we have not fought back. We have seen the proudest people in the world become ashamed of success and shy about competing. The very elements that have made America great have been labeled "selfish, greedy, and oppressive." Those elements of our society that produced the greatest standard of living for everyone who lived here are being revisited by Americans. They are the principles of competition with equal rights, not special rights. Principles are goals, not a comparison to reality. We may never reach the pinnacles of our principles, but we must always try.

What happened to America? How did we get so far from the path of greatness that directed us? Did we become so complacent, so arrogant in our achievements, that the enemy just walked in and took over? It seems we just did not recognize the enemy or appreciate his strategy. American socialism is not a religion or even a philosophy; it is a lifestyle. Someone asked what the difference was between a socialist and a communist. A communist is a socialist in a hurry. Socialism is a gradual process on many fronts. It will grow on you like cancer. Communism is the result of a revolution and is very rapid. We are ready for communism, but are defenseless against the onslaught of socialism.

There Are No Great Conspirators Designing the Fall Of the American Culture, But There Is A Lifestyle That Is Contributing To It

The hatred for the rich, multi-culturalism, government dependency, and poor education have been a lifestyles-driven phenomena, coupled with the "victims": Black people, women, teenagers, the elderly, immigrants, the poor, AIDS patients, and students. No one is "responsible," and therefore we have a culture of blame.

In the 1990's we began to see Black men marching on Washington, D.C., women protesting in China, "starving children" marching against Congress and the elderly marching against the budget. Have you noticed that it is all your fault and you are to blame?

Black Americans are still waiting for their forty acres and a mule, women for their equal rights, AIDS victims for more funding, the poor for more aid, and all are placing blame and anger at someone else. Finally the American culture is returning and the "can- do" spirit is rising up in our communities.

Organizations of self-help and personal responsibility are taking the forefront in social directing. The Concerned Women for America, Promise Keepers, and local groups like The Committee To Restore America, are all standing up to be counted and to be responsible. Citizens are taking pride in America and the rights of the individual are being recognized. We have a long way to go after forty years of not fighting back. However, I have seen more battles won and more American spirit than ever.

The American spirit was not dead; it was just asleep. Welcome back, America! Now let's return to our own American lifestyle. As imperfect a people as we are, we can never respect group rights over individual rights. It has been great and I am confident about our future. God bless America!

Even with the so-called "Black church fires," the true spirit of the American population comes shining through. The national attention has now turned to a supposedly increased incident of arson at predominantly Black churches. Moreover, this has also increased calls for action by the civil rights leaders. I have two questions. If someone is burning down churches, is that a civil rights problem or a Christian problem? In addition, are the numbers of church fires increasing over previous years? The number of arson church fires could be growing, or simply reported more often.

News organizations are giving many statistics on the number of fires and type of congregation. It would be very hard to classify a church by its "color," so many of these "Black churches" may not be Black. I contacted the Bureau of Alcohol, Tobacco and Firearms, Arson and Explosive Division- Arson Enforcement Branch, for the accurate number. They have a list of active investigations of predominantly Black churches in the Southeast United States since 1995: twenty-five, in 1995: five, in 1996: twenty. These and the following figures are as of June 7, 1996.

The ATF has investigated 47 church fires since January of 1995. Within that number are 25 Black churches, 8 Jewish synagogues and 14 predominantly White churches. I would imagine there are many more predominantly White churches in America than Black, so 25 Black churches burning to 14 Whites would raise many concerns. We do not know the answer to this question, but we can tell the numbers are not increasing, except this year.

From October 1991 until January 1995, there have been a total of 95 churches burned. This is an average of 30 fires a year. This total included all church fires Black, White and mixed. My computer database lists 266,550 churches and shrines in America with an additional 12,266 organizations. I just do not think 30 fires a year is a national news item with over 278,000 targets.

The real concern is that people are burning down our churches. The color of its congregations is not as important. The response should be from the Christian community, not from the civil rights community. Although arson of Black churches brings up painful memories of the struggles for civil rights in America, we cannot allow a few racists still among us to divide us along religious lines. The Christian community is not organized along racial lines but along theological and spiritual lines. Our services may be segregated by racial lines, but we all have the same faith and hold the same principles. That is why the calls for action by the Christian Coalition, Promise Keepers and other Christian organizations are a welcome sign of unity in the faith.

In addition, of course, with every crisis come the politicians. Bill Clinton used his weekly radio broadcast to show his emotional connection to the recent reports of church fires. He stated, "I have vivid and painful memories of Black churches being burned down in my own state when I was a child." This statement was given with care and emotion--and apparently in complete fantasy. The President has vivid memories of events that just did not happen. Bill Clinton has vividly remembered something that never occurred.

The *Arkansas Democrat-Gazette* of June 3, 1996, reported that the state historian, the president of the Arkansas NAACP, and the former president of the Regular Arkansas Baptist Convention (a group of 530 Black churches) could not recall any church burning in Arkansas during the civil rights period. Do not forget President Clinton also had a vivid memory of not inhaling marijuana during this same period. Maybe Clinton just thought he saw churches burning. I would not like to think our President would use this tragedy to play on the fear and anger of the Klan and the terror of the "Night Raiders" of history. I personally resent the President's disregard of my faith and his flagrant tear at the emotions of Black Americans.

The media reports of church fires have captured the imagination of the country. Stories of predominantly Black congregations being burned out by racist White people have been plentiful. In this book, I have discussed the numbers of fires in 1996 compared to previous years. We have had the new Black Panthers offering protection, Ku Klux Klan offering organization and the government offering more control over our lives. Only the people affected are offering solutions.

The current levels of church fires are not out of the ordinary, nor are they targeted at any racial group. If anything can be learned, it is that hatred of organized religion is not restricted to race or denominations. White and Black churches are burning; even Jewish temples are being torched. We have had arrests of teenagers and church members as well as the local Klan.

Recent wire service reports have covered Ku Klux Klan members charged with church burning in South Carolina. Other reports suggest mentally ill members of burned churches, drunken teenagers, disgruntled members and conspiring pastors may have been involved in many burnings. All of this points to a big non-story for the national news. The fires are not unusual nor are they a trend.

Since January of 1995, 207 churches have burned and 12 desecrated in America. Of the burnings, 39 were found to be accidental. Despite charges of no help from the government, there have been arrests made in 54 of the cases, and 69 people have been taken into custody. Investigations are ongoing in 114 cases. There have been many reports of the 70 Black churches burned since January 1995. Little of the coverage has reported that only a third of these fires are suspected to be racially motivated.

While it is easy to focus on the anger, fear and despair of stories like these, there is another story. It is a story of what happens to a community struck with a disaster. What happens is that communities all over the nation are discovering each other in the midst of tragedy. When a church burns down it affects the entire community, and everyone must respond.

All over America, Americans are responding by volunteering to help each other and rebuild these churches. White congregations are helping Black, and Christians are helping Jews, and the walls that separate us are crumbling in the midst of these fires. Relationships are being forged that will never be broken, and people are coming together on their commonalities rather than dwelling on their differences.

We keep hearing about "multi-culturalism" and all of our differences, but these communities have discovered the ties that bind us. The real stories of these churches burning have been the community efforts to rebuild the social fabric along with the buildings. Communities that grew up separated by racial distrust and fears are now working together side by side. From South Carolina to California, people are disproving the notion that we are a divided nation. From President Clinton and Vice President Al Gore to Newt Gingrich and the Promise Keepers, church rebuilding has been a voluntary reaction to hatred.

White and Black congregations who have never communicated with each other are now worshipping together and rebuilding together. Children are learning to play with each other and seeing their parents working for the community. Out of the tragedy of the fires will rise healthy relationships and love.

We have learned a great lesson: hatred can only destroy and only love can build. The hatred that sought to destroy has only hastened its own destruction. The community did not respond with hatred, suspicion or anger; it responded with love, and love covers a multitude of sins.

Equal Rights, Not Special Rights....The Movement Continues

We have never been one individual or one culture! The beauty of the Black community has always been the diverse cultural aspects of its people. Since slavery began in 1444, African slaves came from different tribes with different languages, traditions and cultures. We were forced into one language and one culture but have always kept some differences. It seems there are some elements in America who still expect us to be predictable and controllable. I hope they handle disappointment well.

The Black Community Today Is Multi-Cultural

There is no "Black Culture." Some Black people like jazz, blues, rap, or gospel music. Some are Christian and some are Muslim. Well, I have news for you! Some are even conservative and some are liberal, some are right-wing and some are left-wing. Someone once said, "It takes two wings to get the plane off the ground."

My question to you is, do you recognize only one wing? Do you purposely seek out only one small section of our community for comments and reactions to current events?

I have heard estimates that there are between 10,000 and 300,000 Black Muslims in America, but Minister Farrakhan is the one to whom the media turns. They ignore the 28,000,000 Black Christians in America.

Seventy percent of the Black population has managed to live above the poverty level, but only those Black Americans in our community on government assistance are portrayed.

With approximately 80% of Black youths graduating from high school, why is our image that of illiterate dropouts?

The conservative movement is the next logical step in

the civil rights movement. Approximately 25-33% of the Black community considers themselves conservative, and more than 50% aren't sure. We are mainstream; we have a long tradition and our opinions are based upon well-thought-out logic.

We are standing up today to declare that we are like any other community in America. Our strength lies in our differences, and the media's nonrecognition of these differences is our weakness.

The Black community is not a tribe, and we have no tribal chief speaking for us. We are a hardy people who not only have survived slavery, but have thrived.

Why is it newsworthy that a group of Black Americans are stating our commitment to families? When did it become news that Black people are not demanding a handout? Who told you that it is strange and different for a group of Black people to desire to participate openly in the American dream and not depend on the "American dreamers" for permission?

White Americans are not criticized or thought of as being odd if they are conservative, right-wing or capitalist. Black people fitting this description are not only criticized, they are considered traitors to their people. Are we stereotyping tens of millions of people? We love America and what it has to offer, and we intend to participate fully in the American culture.

The dream of Martin Luther King was of a country where Americans participate openly in the American dream. We agree with that. Why is that news?

"We are not militant, only confident! Never angry, but aware! Not vicious, but victorious!"

Mason Weaver

We are not going to quietly allow our critics to name-call, spread lies regarding our motives and unjustly criticize our political and social beliefs. We will continue to

respond to the issues affecting our nation, as we will continue to stand for the principles that have made us great.

And we will continue to answer our critics with
"THE TRUTH, RIGHT BETWEEN THE LIES!"

Chapter Seven

Open the Gate, We are Leaving!

"I shall never permit myself to stoop so low as to hate any man." **Booker T. Washington**

On July 1, 1991, President George Bush nominated conservative Justice Clarence Thomas to the U.S. Supreme Court. Unwittingly President Bush had launched the Black conservative movement in America. With Justice Thomas' nomination, the Black tribal chiefs had a fit. They tried everything to discredit and foil his confirmation to the bench.

Black conservatives, who had previously thought they were all alone, witnessed the televised hearings and saw themselves. Black conservative after conservative stepped up to the limelight in defense of Clarence Thomas. Suddenly, Black conservatives in San Diego knew they had friends in Washington. Groups in Houston knew about groups in Memphis. All of the sudden the mirage was broken and a movement was launched. Eventually names like Walter Williams, Thomas Sowell, Star Parker and Ezola Foster became known to the nation.

We would never take the back seat to liberal activism in our community again. Once we understood that we were not alone, we also understood what we were called to do.

Many people like to believe that Clarence Thomas was unqualified to be nominated for the Supreme Court. The argument is invalid and is motivated by his conservative views more than his qualification. If these liberal civil rights leaders were concerned about the age and experience of Justice Thomas, then they should have been equally concerned about General Colin Powell's nomination as Chairman of the Joint Chiefs of Staff.

Both men were relatively young for the job, and that youth restricted the amount of experiences they could have had. However, to argue the qualification of Justice Thomas to replace Thurgood Marshall is not fair to either man.

Justice Marshall was a great leader in the civil rights struggle when the battle was in full attack. His arguments before the Supreme Court and other cases opened the door for people like Justice Thomas to advance. However, once the doors of opportunity were open, Justice Thomas took advantage of them. While Marshall went to Howard Law School, Thomas went to Yale.

It could be argued that Marshall could not have entered Yale Law School. However, if the struggles of Marshall and others opened the door for Black Americans to enter Yale Law School, then the achievement of Clarence Thomas should have been heralded as honoring the life and works of Marshall.

Clarence Thomas could be considered the result of Thurgood Marshall, and they complemented each other. It was ironic and justified to have a man who took advantage of the victory assume the seat of him who won the victory.

A comparison of the qualifications of both men, at the time of their nomination, reveals more similarities than differences. Both men graduated law school around the same age (Marshall at 25 and Thomas at 26), both had distinguished careers working for civil rights groups (one for conservative causes and the other liberal) and both served in lower courts before being nominated to the highest court in the land.

Although Justice Thomas was much younger than Marshall, the times were also different. Both graduated college with honors and had brilliant minds. The detractors of Thomas should be honest enough to admit his conservative views are the real problems they have with him.

On September 30, 1994, hundreds of Americans converged on Houston, Texas for the National Leadership Conference. They came from all over to meet and fellowship with others with similar beliefs. They shared a common frustration of being lone warriors for moral and economic values. These were conservative Americans of slave descent. It was a powerful meeting where no one was whining about the White conspiracy or demanding more handouts. No one was blaming anyone else for the conditions of our community and no one was apologizing for success.

This Was A Group of Black Americans Who Love America, Not for What It Had Been Or Even for What It Is Now, But for What It Could Be

We who gathered in Houston for the National Leadership Conference understood how far America had to go, but we also understood how far it had traveled. There is no other country in the world that offers as much to its people as America. We understood the legacy of slavery and the cruelty of its system. We also understood how America has torn herself apart to change.

It was this legacy that brought us together. After

420 years of a plantation mentality, it was about time.

It is time we declare how the war on poverty has made more of us poor. It is time we abolish a welfare system that creates broken families devoid of self-esteem. It is time we recognize there is something wrong when 10% of the population is having 44% of the abortions. This population is killing its children in the streets and making junkies out of many others.

In Houston, we decided it was time to return to the low-cost, high-quality schools that taught our people skills and respect. We rejected the high-cost, low-quality schools that graduate our children with little self-respect and no future. We believe the term "multi- cultural" really means "divide and conquer" or is another term for "separate but equal."

In Houston We Came Together To Say That Taxing the Wealthy Only Keeps Us From Getting Wealthy

When there is a 10% government set-aside program for us, we are being restricted from 90% of the business opportunities. We want lower taxes, no minimum wage and smaller government. The Federal subsidies, food stamps, AFDC, and 75 other welfare programs look far too much like the plantation for our comfort.

Over four hundred Americans of African slave descent came together to ask questions and make decisions. They gave birth to a new organization tentatively called "Mainstream USA." We are neither Black Americans nor African-Americans; we are mainstream.

However, the meeting was not a social gathering—it was a social awakening. These Black conservatives are no longer alone and unorganized, but operate now in a network of writers, radio talk-show hosts, researchers, spokesmen and mainstream organizations.

We left Texas with a plan as well as a renewed spirit of commitment. We were determined to return home and challenge the defeatist attitudes within our communities. We would never allow the voice of hopelessness to go unchallenged before us. We were energized just by meeting each other and encouraged by the overwhelming offers to come to each other's aid.

I met other talk-show hosts who agreed to share information and guests, magazine editors who would print our stories, and many interesting people to call upon when help was needed.

There was one thing we all felt could be done. If we could simply increase the number of Black Republican voters in the 1994 elections, we would have accomplished two things. If we could increase the Republican share of the Black voter turnout to over 10%, we would completely end the Democrat control over this country. The second thing we would accomplish would be an evaluation of how our message is being received by Black Americans.

We went home and waited for the 1994 elections, and all we heard from the media was about the "angry White males."

However, what really happened in 1994 was a major shift in Black voting patterns. The usual Republican share of 5 to 8% of the Black vote swelled to 12% nationwide. It was the largest percentage in decades, and a major reason for the Republican landslide of that year. Looking at individual races shows more of a picture of the strong Republican showing in the Black communities. California Republican Governor Wilson received 21% of the Black votes, Ohio Republican Governor George Voinovich received 40%.[8] It was the same everywhere. Major shifts in Black voting patterns should have been the news. We won in 1994 and came into our own. Too bad the media was looking for angry White men instead.

Kwanzaa and Other Substitutes for Reality

The winter season is a special time of the year for me. First there is the *make-believe* celebration of "Kwanzaa" in December, then honoring Dr. Martin Luther King's birthday in January, and the month-long culmination of "Black History Month" for February. As a Black American, this season is a time of reflection on heritage and honor. It is a time of reflection on the character and dignity that has served the Black community for so many years.

The struggle within this segment of the U.S. population is both external and internal. We have suffered from self-hatred while seeking self-respect. We have been considered both lazy and hard-working by the same people, simultaneously. Our leaders call for separation, integration and revolution in the same breath. In our past era where reading and writing were illegal, education was next to freedom in importance. However, today, education is left in the hands of the new plantation owners. The results have been the same: less success and more dependency on the master.

As America begins the next Black History Month,

let us resist the temptation to look only at the negatives. We could talk about the beatings, lynching, rapes and murders. One could speak about the lost, stolen or deflected opportunities and hopes of a people. However, while we look at how bad it was, let us take heart in the achievements of our people. Success has always been difficult, especially during times of slavery and legal discrimination. From 1619 until 1865 Black Americans both survived and thrived. Some examples of accomplishments during the days of slavery would include:

*The first general institution organized and managed by Black people was the Free African Society of Philadelphia, founded April 12, 1787.

*Alexander Lucius Twilight was elected to the Vermont legislature in 1836 and was the first Black American elected to public office as well as the first Black to graduate from an American college in 1823.

*The Black actor James Hewlett played the role of Othello in 1821 and Ira Aldridge won international renown for the same role in 1833.

*The American Insurance Company of Philadelphia became the first Black-owned insurance company in 1810.

*The first Black physician was ex-slave James Derham in 1783, and the first Black lawyer was Macon B. Allen of Maine, in 1843.

*The Freedom's Journal became the first Black-owned newspaper, March 16, 1827, in New York.

*Phillis Wheatley was the first Black American author and first major poet. Her book, *Poems on Various Subjects, Religious and Moral,* published in 1773, was the second book published by an American woman.[9]

If Black Americans can accomplish these goals under the weight of slavery, what can be done now? If a Black person could obtain a Ph.D. when it was illegal to read or write, certainly we can conquer high school in the inner cities. Then there were no harsher times to be a Black person, no greater hazards to overcome. Now there are no legal barriers facing us, no overwhelming organized efforts to stop us—at least not as these heroes faced.

Now To Our Legacy, Now To Our Responsibility As A People, Culture And Nation

You honor the past in memory, and you honor the future by action! Let us continue to build a country on forgiveness, courage and pride. We must honor the sacrifices of those who did the impossible, in spite of the intolerable, and suffered the insufferable.

We owe it to them to stop whining and complaining about who has done us wrong. Stand up on history and recognize that no one can stop the American spirit. We owe it to them to make it here in America. The greatest honor is success. Honor your past and your future.

Kwanzaa: Symbolism Over Substance

Increasingly Black Americans are embracing the Kwanzaa celebration and festival. Why? What is the need to recognize a made-up holiday with false traditions? It is because of emotion. The community has been told it is a "Black thing" and therefore it must be honored.

Now, do not get me wrong, I have no problem in remembering my past or honoring traditions. I have a degree in Black History, I speak Swahili and had

acquired an African name long before it became politically correct. However, let us get serious—traditions are for memories, not for made-up holidays.
Kwanzaa is a make believe story full of errors and
falsehoods.

With such a rich heritage and history, why do we
celebrate the fantasy world of a college professor
from the radical 1960's? Professor Ron Karenga
made up Kwanzaa in 1961 to counter the Western
celebration of Christmas. Dr. Karenga made up the
word, made up its definition, and then made up the
elements we recognize today as "traditions." First,
"Kwanzaa" does not spell "first fruits" in Swahili or
any other language.

When I interviewed Dr. Karenga a few years ago,
he admitted that the word was changed from the
Swahili word "Kwanza" to "Kwanzaa" because he
needed seven letters to represent his seven children.
Because I spoke Swahili (and he apparently did not)
Dr. Karenga was forced to admit that the word
"Kwanza" was a Swahili adverb for "first," and he
added the extra "a" and "fruits" because it fit his
story. And for all of you who wish to celebrate "first
fruits," the proper Swahili noun would be "Limbuko,"
which would have given Dr. Karenga his seven letters for his children had he understood the language.

My question is, why celebrate this make-believe
holiday anyway? With the rich history and heritage
of Africa and Black people in America, why not remember what we have accomplished with facts instead of celebrating a fantasy? You could celebrate
the historical defeat of the Roman army by the Ethio-
pians or Hannibal's invasion of Europe. One could
commemorate the great library at Timbuktu or the

engineering feat of the pyramids.

Then there are the historical feats of Black Americans, both the well-known and the never-to-be-known. Benjamin Bannaker's redesign of our Capital from memory, Crispus Attucks, the first man to die in the American Revolution, or the scientific genius of E.J. McCoy (the "Real McCoy") should be honored. We could celebrate the brave adventure of Harriet Tubman's underground railroad or perhaps the unblemished record of the Tuskegee Airmen of World War II.

Juneteenth! Juneteenth is here! What is Juneteenth? Every year about the beginning of June, there are celebrations around the country with festivals and picnics, embracing Juneteenth. The NAACP will have its annual picnic and celebrations, and people will continue to ask the question, what is Juneteenth? I have heard many answers and most are incorrect. Even the "official" explanation raises more questions than it answers, but I will try to explain the history and tradition of this Black American holiday called Juneteenth.

Officially, it is a remembrance of events that happened the second week of June 1865. On or about June 13, Union General Gordon Granger arrived with Federal troops outside Galveston Island, Texas, liberating the 200,000 slaves of the region. Earlier, on January 1, 1863, President Abraham Lincoln issued the Emancipation Proclamation. From this point, history is excused and fantasy begins.

The story continues that it took two years for the word of the Emancipation to reach the slaves in Texas. The cruel slave master did not tell the Texas slaves about it and kept them working until the Union troops showed up. The resulting celebration of freedom was called "Emancipation Day" and the timing was June thirteenth through the nineteenth. It soon became known as Juneteenth (13th-19th).

While the events concerning General Granger were true, it did not take two years for word of the Emancipation to reach Texas; it just took two years for the troops to show up. The Emancipation Proclamation did not free any slaves, and none were freed until the war was over. Why would anyone expect the slaveholders in rebellion to free their slaves because Mr. Lincoln said so? There was a war going on, and the South was not listening to Lincoln.

The Southern States had declared their independence from Washington and formed their own government. They took orders from their own President and received power from their Congress and courts. Just as we declared independence from Great Britain, the South had to defend itself against the Union. No slaves were free in the South on Mr. Lincoln's say-so because the South was not under his control.

If the United States President declared all prisoners in Mexico's jails were now free, would they be? It would not matter until the 101st Airborne marched into Mexico City to enforce the order. A careful reading of the Emancipation Proclamation will point out how specific Lincoln's order was. Not only were certain slaves of certain states declared free but even parts of certain counties. Only those slaves in the states who were in rebellion were free. Slaves in states controlled by Mr. Lincoln kept their slaves, and even states that would rejoin the Union could have kept slaves.

We get the impression that the Union troops were like the liberating armies of World War II. Nevertheless, the Union troops placed slaves in "contraband camps," because they were still considered property. If the Emancipation Proclamation freed slaves, why would we still need to pass the 13th and 14th amendments to the Constitution?

Lincoln was a great man and a great President, but what freed the slaves was the struggle for freedom fought long before the war began. It was John Brown at Harper's Ferry, Harriet Tubman's railroad, Stowe's writings and Frederick Douglass' oratory. Freedom was won by the Black troops and the White troops who died for it. Freedom was won as it has always been won by self-sacrifice of those oppressed. It is very sad that some would like to distort history with stories. The truth is, if Lincoln freed the slaves, then we are still slaves, because no one is free until he frees himself.

We Should Honor Our Traditions With Real Historical Events Like "Juneteenth," Martin Luther King Day, Or the End of Apartheid

In this search for our African past let us remember one thing. Not only did Africans come here as slaves, but the continent was also colonized and Africans became slaves on their own lands.

Our people were held as slaves in their own country by colonists. Others were kidnapped to foreign lands as slaves. Today, in spite of the harshness of the slave trade and the cruelty of Jim Crow and segregation, the descendants of the slaves in America have done quite well. We are the healthiest, most literate and most influential group of Black people in the world. We have more education, money, freedom and power than any other. Despite the harshness of American life for Black people, we have thrived and should be proud. I honor the past as history, not fantasy; Kwanzaa is fantasy.

Now some of you only want to look for the negative because some of you are comfortable being the victims. But I have read my history and know who I am, where I came from, and where I am going. I have discovered that if the slave master could not destroy my spirit, if Jim Crow could not quench my dreams and if racist Americans could not keep me down, there is no force on earth capable of doing these things—except one, me! If I believe I am a victim, then I am.

Politics Is Politics, For All Races

As we enter election seasons, let us keep something in mind. There are only a few criteria by which we should elect a candidate. Constitutionally the President has little authority over most of our lives, but this authority is almost absolute in some areas. The decision on sending our troops into battle and appointing lifetime judges over us has become the absolute domain of Presidents.

Although the Constitution grants overview and even decision-making to Congress, we have been unable to stop most actions of Presidents in these two areas. Therefore, the voting decision should be weighed by character. I have only two questions for each of our candidates: under what circumstances will you go to war, and what are your criteria for selecting Federal judges?

If you examined the major tragedies in our country's history you can easily find the judges of long-gone Presidents playing a pivotal role. The Dred Scott decision, Brown versus the Board of Education, Roe versus Wade and the problems with California's Proposition 187 all stem from judges left to us by past Presidents and governors. Long after we have corrected the mistakes of elections, their influence still affects our lives.

The decisions of Abraham Lincoln lasted a hundred years after his death. I served in Vietnam long after Kennedy and Johnson were out of office, and the Iron Curtain of Europe fell after Ronald Reagan had returned to California. The decision of electing a President will have effects on our economy and culture long after the official leaves office.

It is not important how charismatic the candidate is. How impressive his speech delivery is or how caring he is should not move us. The character of this person should reflect our character because his character will affect our lives for years to come.

President Clinton Has A History Of Not Caring for the Military Or Serving In It

Clinton has made no apologies for past statements and actions indicating his disdain for the military service. Therefore, we should not have been surprised when he used military officers assigned to the White House in ways insulting to their position. Shortly after his inauguration, Clinton degraded the fine officers by having them serve as waiters for his State dinners and other functions at the White House.

President Clinton sent your sons and daughters to Bosnia to help with his reelection campaign, and no one seemed to care about character. It is not enough that he failed in Haiti and Somalia, it was not good enough that he opened the military to practicing homosexuals, but then he used the greatest fighting force in the world as waiters at the White House. Our troops served in Bosnia as targets, mine-clearing experts, and road builders. These deployments were little more than campaign ploys.

We are already set to suffer well into this new millennium because of his court appointments. This has fueled a renewed call for term limits of Federal judges. What we need are more decisive and selective electors who will stop placing people in office for frivolous reasons. This government solves every problem by taking more control over our businesses, private property, and lives.

Have we seen enough yet? Did we like the Clinton Health Care Plan, tax cuts and broken promises on a balanced budget? Can anyone really be impressed with this government's education policy? Are you prepared to see your troops under the control of the United Nations? Will you tolerate more government control over your homes and business? Are you willing to follow a President with no direction and little integrity? It seems to me that we should all ask ourselves the question "Who will he nominate to the courts?" and "Under which circumstance will he commit our soldiers to battle?" An informed electorate should consider these questions.

Sure, President Clinton is a dynamic, charismatic person. However, the office of the President of the United States is not a figurehead position. This position represents the morality and culture of the American people. This person will lead (or mislead) the free world, and we are solely responsible for the choice.

It is one of the most important decisions a self-governing people will make. We should not make our decision on looks, personality, or the sensitivity of the candidate. The election of the President should not be a popularity contest selected on the show-manship of the official. This office should be a re-flection of the heart and soul of the American people.

Elected Officials Should Be Chosen Based Upon Our Combined Faiths, Loves, Fears and Solemn Commitment To Principles

If we elect a President for any other reason we are doing a great disservice to our ancestors and our children. Our ancestors left us with the rights and privileges of a free society, and our children depend on us to reserve and preserve these rights and privi-leges for them. Choose a President like you would choose the legal guardian of your children. Choose wisely or be governed foolishly.

President Clinton's 1996 State of the Union ad-dress was something for everybody. It became clear, early in the telecast, that the President was in full campaign mode, "talking from the right but govern-ing from the left." He promised everyone everything, and if you listened carefully, he did not promise any-one anything.

The President wanted a balanced budget but could not get one, even when his party controlled Con-gress. Instead, we got a retroactive tax increase on everyone, sparing not even the dead. Our President stated the "era of big government was over!" Does that mean he amended his health care proposals, which would have controlled 7% of our economy from Washington? The President declared his support for a balanced budget but vetoed the only balanced budget submitted to the White House in 30 years. His call for a balanced budget was only rhetoric as he excluded such budget-busting programs like Medicaid, Social Security, Welfare and Education.

President Clinton wanted us to understand that he heard our demands for less government but insisted we not go back to the days when Americans "went at it alone." However, the partnership he refers to is a burden, not a help. This partnership is unequal and less productive; it has little to contribute and takes more control over our business. What the President means by "partnership" is "control."

President Clinton took credit for reducing the number of Federal employees and the national debt. Of course, most of those "Federal employees" are members of our military, not the bloated social bureaucracy. He did such a great job of military reduction that we could not deploy a few thousand troops from within Europe to Bosnia without calling up the reserves. I believe it is a disturbing revelation when this country cannot quickly send a small detachment of troops a few hundred miles without the reserves.

In his speech, the President suggested the Russian military no longer has missiles pointed at American cities. Other than the President, does anyone else want to bet on that? How many of you are willing to believe there are no Russian submarines patrolling the Pacific Ocean with nuclear missiles programmed for Camp Pendleton? What American could believe the threat from Russian bombers is not real for the Eastern Seaboard? How could the

President assure us that no Russian mobile launchers were sitting in Eastern Europe aimed at us? We were just supposed to trust our President that there was no threat.

Are we this gullible? Did anyone believe his long admiring look during the State of the Union Address to Mrs. Clinton was spontaneous? Perhaps he is in love with his wife and appreciates her, but everyone understood that gesture as an act of support for her legal troubles. These insincere emotional symbolic poses by the President are what made people doubt his character and sincerity. I do not know what is more frightening—a President who believes he can fool all of the people all of the time, or the 40+ percent of us who appeared fooled all of the time.

We waited until the election to truly tell if the people would reclaim our country. Only the elections could tell us if we were to follow a great storyteller or return to the great story. The great story is of a people who do not depend upon government, but upon themselves. This people had a choice between equal rights and special rights, and could have stood for independence, not co-dependence. This is the choice America now faces: symbolism over substance.

Who are our heroes—a President who refused to serve our country, or Army specialist Michael New who refused to serve the United Nations?

Michael New is the U.S. military hero who refused to disobey his oath to America. He was ordered to take off his U.S. uniform and put on the uniform of the United Nations. He was expected to follow the orders of a foreign military officer and serve a world government institution. Michael New considered himself an American military man, not a "world peace keeper," and refused the order to change uniforms.

"The era of big government is over!" These words, spoken by President Clinton during his 1996 State of the Union Address, were a hopeful sign. If big government liberals felt the need to campaign on this theme, then maybe it really is over. Since I am the type who considers what you do as more important that what you say, I am not convinced Clinton really wanted a smaller government. But he certainly believed YOU wanted a smaller government.

Character Should Play An Important Role In all Elections

The American people must decide between someone who speaks well and someone who can lead. We can choose based upon the ability to identify problems and the person's history of solving them. If these were the criteria, any one of the Republican candidates should have easily beaten Clinton in 1992 and 1996.

We should have chosen based upon a history of keeping promises and not the ability to make promises. However, we did not use this criteria. Unfortunately, many of us do not even know who our elected officials are. Recent surveys and polls have found Americans ignorant of the political and social issues. Apparently, we cannot decide which major party is conservative and which is liberal, whether we want to cut or raise taxes, or even the names of our elected representatives. Surveys pointed out a major confusion and apathy among the voters. No wonder we blame "politicians" for political troubles instead of the "policies" of political parties.

We could blame this on the poor political knowledge taught in school civics classes, broken promises of the past or both parties being too close in philosophies. Nevertheless, I put the blame on us, the American people. We have spent too much of our time watching O.J. instead of Washington. ESPN is more popular than C-SPAN, and MTV controls more of our attention and loyalty than NET (National Empowerment Television). This is somewhat understandable, as entertainment will always be more appealing than education, but education will always be more important than entertainment.

Our children can recite any rap song, but not *"America the Beautiful."* Everyone knew that Magic Johnson would return, but not many knew Michael New refused to go. While Magic Johnson wanted to serve the public in the NBA, army specialist Michael New refused to serve the United Nations under foreign command. I will admit, Johnson is more entertaining, but New is far more inspiring. Who is the real hero and role model—an athlete returning to what he loves for glory, or a soldier giving up what he loves for honor?

It gives me courage when I see individuals and groups begin to stand up for what they believe and daring to change things. From parents in the Escondido, California, school district fighting to keep math taught, to the bipartisan uproar against Michael New's court-martial, the American spirit is beginning to stir. However, unless we are willing to sacrifice and even lose what we have, we will always fall short.

Ask yourself a question, do we need more Magic Johnsons to entertain us or Michael News to expose our souls?

Are we going to be one government, controlled from outside this country, or do you believe the world needs a strong America? If you believe in a strong America, then you must continue to stir. We have a long way to go, but we must go.

Government cannot solve our social problems. Government has never solved our social problems; it has only made them worse. Only the American people can resolve social and economical problems, because we are a self-governed people. "WE, THE PEOPLE" ended slavery, Jim Crow, and the Vietnam War, won women's suffrage, and brought down the Iron Curtain. Only "WE, THE PEOPLE" can end racism, poverty, and crime and educate our children. Big government is a burden.

Who would have thought Long Beach would have fallen before Hong Kong?

Clinton said that big government was over! However, if big government is over, what will take its place--"big world government?" It seems like our nation is being surrendered to enemies for no real reason. Why is our competitive spirit and the will to be winners becoming undesirable social traits? With strange trade agreements and treaties, American culture is being sold onto another plantation and we may all soon be slaves.

I have never thought slavery was motivated by hatred against Africans or Black people. It was tried on many other people first, including Europeans and American Indians. Slavery was motivated by control, not racism. The current surrender of our economy and sovereignty is an issue of power and who wields it.

While we are worried about the CIA and the FBI, someone is stealing away our very country. If we keep looking at ourselves as different cultures, others will instill their culture on us. There is no reason to destroy the plantation; it is better to own it.

If Communism has been defeated, then why do I see so many Communists?

The last time I saw Communists carrying AK47 weapons, I was serving in South Vietnam. I must admit having mixed emotions witnessing the proud warship of Communist China tied up to the proud USS Constellation. Then I saw the picture of the Chinese Navy Admiral guarded by a young sailor with his AK47 rifle.

I know times have changed, but have the Communists changed? Was this the same ship that participated in exercises off Taiwan in the summer of 1997? Was this the same Chinese warship that U.S. carriers like the USS Constellation confronted near Taiwan that summer? Was this the same Chinese military that warned us of their ability to "strike Los Angeles?"

We gave Gorbachev part of the Presidio military base in San Francisco, the United Nations flag is flying in many U.S. government locations, and now we have the Communist Chinese government buying politicians and moving in on the Port of Long Beach.

Not only are they establishing themselves at Long Beach and visiting San Diego, but the Chinese government has major developments other places in America. From major retail developments in Arkansas (where else?), to special docking privileges near U.S. bases, the Chinese are moving fast at winning the economics game.

They are already quickly overtaking Japan as a leading trading partner with the U.S. and have learned their lessons well from Japan. China seems to believe free trade means they are free to trade their product openly in American markets, but feel free to close their markets to our products. For giving lip service to controlling their piracy of our intellectual property and demanding we give up patent rights and trade secrets, one must ask what are we getting for the deal?

Are we getting a better relationship, dialog, or a better understanding of this giant nation? Do we get a reduction of the tension between China and Taiwan? NO! We get heightened tension and more pressure to surrender our friends and allies.

Just days after the Communists left San Diego, days after the Vice President and Newt Gingrich arrived back from Tiananmen Square, the Chinese were back to threats and intimidation.

While Vice President Al Gore was toasting the Chinese leadership, the Clinton Administration was insisting on a U.N. resolution criticizing China. Bill Richardson, the U.S. ambassador to the U.N. in New York, was insisting that China "continued to commit widespread and well-documented human rights abuses." Ambassador Richardson is a member of President Clinton's cabinet and stated that the United Nations' Human Rights Commission recognized human rights violations of Communist China. China argued that no country's human rights record is perfect.

Of course, no one is asking China's record to be perfect-just consistent with normal human dignity and generally-accepted behavior. This rebuke by the

Clinton administration may temper the outcry of China's funding of the Democratic National Committee and other campaign irregularities. However, it seems clear that the U.N.'s 15-nation European Union was not united on its annual bid to condemn China. Therefore, any open attack on China in the U.N. could only be for show. The 53-member commission, led by France, did not vote to condemn. Therefore, Clinton can criticize the human rights violations of China, quell the opposition to Gore's visit and welcome the Communist sailors to the San Diego Zoo.

If Clinton really wanted to take aim at China's human rights violations, why not use Al Gore? Gore was in China with the world press watching and was silent on the subject. At the same time Newt Gingrich visited China and told the Chinese that America would defend Taiwan. The Communist government response was predictable. Taiwan was an "internal" problem, and we should mind our own business. Clinton did not back up Newt; White House spokesman Mike McCurry told reporters that Gingrich was "speaking for himself." That is fine and dandy, but who is speaking for America?

Free Willie 1

"Free Willie 1" is over! The taxpayers of California are finally rid of Willie Brown and his-tax-and spend, back-room, good-old-boy tactics. Liberals are an endangered species, and Willie Brown has been under the feeding and care of taxpayers so long, he may have lost the ability to care for himself. It was appropriate and humane to first free him to the natural habitat that spawned him, San Francisco. There he can frolic around with the other liberals and enjoy

143

the company of other endangered species like union bosses, unproductive teachers, non-caring bureaucrats, the liberal press and big money special-interest groups.

The conclusion of this epic adventure was longer than expected. The voters thought the nightmare was over in 1994 when they voted for a Republican majority in the California State Assembly. However, the combination of politicians addicted to power and independent-thinking Republicans made for a final show by the entertainer Willie Brown. Again, he dazzled us with his wit and maneuverability. Again, the master of the deal proved effective. However, the people of California decided to finally govern themselves without dirty tricks and under-the-table attempts to deny their wishes.

The Day After California Republicans Took Over, There Was An Exodus Of Documents From the California Assembly Office Building

This was stopped by alert Republican staff members who noticed private cars loading up boxes after hours. It took a call to the police and the seizure of dumpsters and garbage trucks to rescue the documents Democrats were trying to remove. These files, now in the hands of the Justice department, suggest a secret political arm of the Democratic party was at work in Sacramento under taxpayers' funding.

Campaign literature, letterhead, memos and phone logs all indicate an organized political machine, acting illegally on taxpayers' time. This acting was done with our money to keep Democrats in power. This is neither new nor surprising, and neither is the little attention paid by the media.

As Willie Brown became the darling of the press, they followed him into his sanctuary of San Francisco. There were far more stories in California newspapers covering the inauguration of Willie Brown as chief groundskeeper (oh, I mean mayor) of San Francisco than the dumpster full of papers found in Sacramento.

Willie Brown is now out, but we must put a hedge about our political philosophy to guard against his return in another executive position. We also need to guard against the return of "Willie-like" politicians—who think political power should be used for control and oppression.

What kind of leader was Willie Brown? Some will say he was a brilliant public servant using his unmatched skills to secure influence and control over the Assembly agenda for the good of the people. Others consider him a symbol of arrogance and intolerance with no patience for anything that would not directly benefit him.

Both may be true or neither could be true, but ask yourself this question: How did California benefit from his tenure as Speaker of the Assembly? Are Californians better off now? Are jobs more secure, taxes better spent, or children educated more effectively? Since Willie Brown became Speaker, did respect for politicians increase to match his income?

Who was better off—Californians or Willie Brown? Who had more to show for his fourteen years of leading our Assembly? Regulations, taxes, fees, and restrictions caused businesses to flee this state like there was a plague here. Republican Tom McClintock once stated that only politicians could cause people to prefer the Arizona and Nevada deserts to the Golden State. People are having trouble planning for their future, and families cannot plan for retirement.

Well, the killer whale has been removed and we have quite a mess to clean up. However, we are pioneers and we love a challenge.

With the re-election of President Clinton and the most scandalous administration in history, we were guaranteed endless hearings, trials, etc. Then we hoped the sequal of "Free Willie 2" would come through indictment or impeachment. Perhaps it still will, but for now Willie can spend his time rafting down the Whitewater river in Arkansas.

The Party For the Rich Or the Party For the Poor

While I was a student at Berkeley and Merritt College in Oakland, CA, I continued to hear professors and students claim that the Democrats were the party "for the poor" and Republicans were the party "for the rich." As I have said previously, I had to decide which philosophy I wanted to accept. Democrats truly believed that their power and influence came from giving services to the poor, so it seemed logical that they would want to create as many poor as possible. If the Democrats believed that the more prosperous you became the more you voted Republican, wouldn't that explain their eagerness to raise taxes and burden businesses?

It seems like the Democrats were always taking from those mean "rich" people to help the poor. They had great programs for you if you did not want to become wealthy.

Now the Republican Party understands that its

power and influence come from people who have the hope of obtaining, and maintaining, wealth. The more prosperous a community, the greater its tendency to vote Republican. It became quite clear to me as a young college student that Republicans wanted as many of us wealthy as possible, because it gave them power.

So, which party did I want to support—one that wanted to take care of me, or one that wanted me to take care of myself? Boy, I had some thinking to do. However, that was not the real question.

I Had Studied History In College and I Knew That the Republican Party Was Founded By the Abolitionists To End Slavery

It was the party of Lincoln and the party of Frederick Douglass. It was the party supported in principle by Harriet Tubman and the other freedom fighters of that era. Should I join the party of the slave master, the party that fought to keep Black people on the plantation, or the party that fought to open the gate and said it was OK to leave the plantation?

The original home for freed Black Americans was with the Republican party. It was the party that swept Black people into office all over the South after the Civil War. It was the party the Democrats forced Black people out of. The Democrats forced Black ex-slaves to reregister back to the party of the slave master. It was not until the early 1930's that the first Black person was elected to a Democrat office. Black Republicans served right after the Civil War. The Republican party is our home.

Black voters have had problems with Republicans as well as Democrats, but our history is with the Republican party. Problems began immediately after the Civil War when Frederick Douglass urged then President Johnson to allow former slaves to vote. Johnson opposed this and was generally against Black suffrage. However, it did not stop Black elections in the deep South, nor the violent reactions of several Democrats and former slave owners.

Lerone Bennett Jr. published *Before the Mayflower*, which chronicles the actions of the Democratic party against Black voters.

1. May 1-3, 1866, White Democrats and police attacked Black Americans and Whites in Memphis, killing 46 and wounding 70. Many homes were burned.

2. July 30, 1866, just one year after the end of the Civil War, White Democrats and police attacked Black and White Republicans in New Orleans. Forty people were killed and 150 wounded.

3. On the same day abolitionist David Walker's son Edward became the first Black to sit in the legislature of an American state in the post-Civil War era. On July 30, 1866, he was elected to the Massachusetts Assembly from the town of Boston.

4. May 20-21, 1868, the Republican National Convention was held in Chicago, marking the national debut of Black politicians.

5. September 19, 1868, White Democrats attacked demonstrators in Georgia, killing nine Black people.

6. June 5-6, 1872, the Republican National Convention in Philadelphia witnessed the first time Black people addressed a major national convention. These three individuals were Elliott, chairman of the South

Carolina delegation; Rainey, of South Carolina; and Lynch of Mississippi.

7. January 17, 1874, Democrats took control of the Texas government by armed force and ended Racial Reconstruction in Texas.

8. August 30, 1874, Democrats killed over 60 Black and White citizens in Louisiana.[10]

Furthermore, in December of 1874, 75 Republicans were killed by Democrats. On July 4, 1875, several Black people were killed again by Democrats, and it goes on and on. Finally Black voters were forced to register Democrat, and that began control of the Black community by the previous slave master.

Once we were part of the Democrat party, Black landowners lost their property, Black voters lost voting rights, sharecropping began and there was an absence of education. Now the Democrat party is still controlling our community with nothing to offer except slavery. It is about time we throw off the shackles of the slave master, stop looking toward him to help us and find our own way.

America In General Is Now Suffering From the Philosophy and Lifestyle Of A Socialist Party That Must Take Care of Dependent Children

We are not the pet of White America and we are not the White man's burden. We are not some kind of endangered species that must be managed by the government. White America may owe us a debt from the slave trade, but they will never give us more than we can earn. The greatest revenge is success.

Let us compete with America and with the world.

Let us forgive the past and work together for the future. We owe too much to the suffering of our ancestors to give up on America.

It is our country; we have earned it and now we must stop the dependency to the master. I know it is a frightening concept, but as a people, it is a journey we have longed to make. Our ancestors prayed for this day. They longed for the opportunity we have. We have now been presented with answers to our prayers. The Red Sea has parted and some are still longing for Pharaoh's comfort. The war is over and some are still fighting it, but it is time to move on.

It will take courage beyond what we think we can do. It is up to us, not them; it is now, not later. We have become comfortable in our misery and familiar with the plantation system, but we must go forward, because **It's OK to Leave the Plantation!**

Conclusion

I can clearly remember one Sunday after church in 1964. My mother was listening to a radio program of a Black man giving a speech. At first, I thought it was just another Sunday afternoon radio preacher, but this man was familiar to me. His voice was forceful like many other preachers; his delivery was as polished as any other good Black southern preacher, but something was different about him. As the son and grandson of preachers, I had heard many of them in the past, and I knew this guy, but I could not place him. My mother told me his name was Dr. Martin Luther King Jr., and he was talking about this bill in Congress called the Civil Rights Act.

It was the first time I can remember hearing about the 1964 Civil Rights Act, and it was the first spark of my involvement in politics. I knew who Dr. King was and now remembered where I had first heard him speak. The previous year he had led a large march on Washington, D.C., and delivered a great speech called "I Have a Dream." That was also the year four children died in a church bombing and Dr. King gave their eulogy. I was aware of the struggles, marches, boycotts and protests, but this was the first time I could remember the government deciding to do something about it.

The 1964 Civil Rights Act was the foundation of how I would judge politics in general and political parties and philosophies in particular. I did not know what a Democrat or Republican was; I could not tell a conservative from a liberal. What I did have was a sense of honesty and fairness; I knew right from wrong.

Recently I had to go back and research what really happened during the Congressional debate and voting on the Act. I was beginning to get the impression that I must have been dreaming because what I remembered was not what was being reported to have happened. During the debate over California Proposition 209 (the Affirmative Action proposition), I continued to hear people speak about the 1964 Civil Rights Act as if it belonged only to the Democratic Party. You would get the impressions that Republicans all voted against it and fought its passage vigorously. However, I remembered the Act as a bipartisan victory and celebrated it as such at the time.

A higher percentage of Republicans voted for the Act than Democrats, and it could not have passed without a large Republican support base. When the Act passed into law, 62% of the House Democrats and 69% of Senate Democrats supported it. Compare this support to the 79% of House Republicans and 80% of the Senate Republicans voting for the Act. You will see that percentage-wise, Republicans supported the Act in greater numbers than Democrats did. (Since Democrats outnumbered Republicans, I thought looking at the percentage was the only fair analysis.)

The 1964 Civil Rights Act was not a Democrat or Republican issue; it was an issue of principles, and it was supported overwhelmingly by both houses and both parties. Published in the August 9, 1964, edition of the <u>Los Angeles Times</u> was an article titled "Democrats Debate GOP Credit for Rights Act." It stated, "Democratic strategists are debating whether to write into their party platform a statement giving congressional Republicans full credit for their role in enacting the 1964 civil rights law."

Apparently, this idea did not make it into the 1964 Democratic Platform, but the consideration was there. The Platform does address the bipartisan efforts of fighting racial discrimination when it included "resting upon a national consensus expressed by the overwhelming support of both parties." As I remembered it, the platform, both parties and the country understood the nation could not impair the rights of any American but must affirm the rights of us all.

Four years later, on April 4, 1968, a bullet would shatter the dream of King. It is still to be determined if that bullet shattered the dream for America. It was on that same date I traveled from the foothills of the Ozark Mountains to Saint Louis, Missouri, to sign up for the U.S. Navy. I had dropped out of high school because the school officials wanted to keep me from graduating. I was determined to finish in the military and get away from that town.

When I arrived back to my hometown that day it was after 6 o'clock in the evening. The bus stop was located at the "Bus Café," the small restaurant downtown. My family had recently moved to this town, and we had been warned about places not welcoming Black people. The Bus Café was reportedly one of those establishments. I must admit to never seeing or hearing anything in that establishment that would give proof of the rumors. I was always served food and treated properly. I was not served gladly but I was served.

Unlike the local theater, which did not welcome Black people and you knew it, the Bus Café seemed opened to this new integration policy of the nation.

As I called home for a ride, a schoolmate walked up to me with the news of Dr. King's death. This White boy seemed almost gleeful as he told me Dr. King had been murdered in Memphis, Tennessee.

I was shocked that such a thing could happen. I decided to walk home, since I had a lot of thinking to do. On the way home many thoughts crossed my mind. Could I serve a country that did not respect me? Was this my America? At eighteen, I had already witnessed personal racial discrimination by school officials, businesses, law enforcement and private citizens. Now they had murdered the man of peace. Now the voices of war had no counter voice. War it would be.

Now we have won the war! The war for dignity, honor and freedom has been won. Are we prepared to win the victory? Why are so many people so unhappy with victory?

Have you ever wondered why the liberals seem so unhappy? When was the last time you saw Jesse Jackson, Ted Kennedy or Dick Gephart happy? They are always complaining, arguing or protesting. That is how they operate. If you believed the liberal view of your world, it would make you very miserable.

When I was in college, I believed the liberal idea of me. I believed that no matter how educated I was, how hard I tried or how good I was, I could not make it in America. Another man, a White man, had all the power over my family and me.

Think about it; if you believed this, why go to school? Why get up for work since the White man is conspiring to keep you down? Why try? In fact, the White man owes me something, and I am going to stay right here until he gives it to me. Many of my militant friends at Berkeley became angry and depressed. Why wouldn't they? Grown men thought they were totally helpless to take charge of their future. I saw many of them justify violence and crime. After all, if you thought you were powerless you could justify robbing, stealing and even drug use, because the White man has you down.

That feeling of helplessness motivates riots and dissolution. And it kills the spirit of freedom and individual action. I felt that despite the power of the White man, the only power great enough to keep me down was myself. Only if I believed it could it affect me. I had seen and read about far too many victories over the system to let the system win.

I still believed in the great White conspiracy, but saw how powerless it was. I knew from my history who I was and what I could do.

Whether the White man hated me did not matter if he conspired; then let him. What mattered was the question of what I could do with what I had control over. I had schoolbooks in my hand and could read; I controlled that. I could go to school and hear the lectures; I had control of that. The White man could not keep me from preparing myself to compete against him; I controlled that. So I went to school, studied, read, and attended the lectures. I prepared myself for the competition ahead. I knew my greatest weapon was the truth.

Is truth relative or absolute? Can truth be found or is it created? Is truth the same as belief? When I hear the term "the truth as I see it" I shudder with frustration. The truth is not as you see it; the truth is as it is. Truth is not relative; it is absolute. Truth is eternal and unchangeable and does not submit itself to the thoughts, hopes or actions of man. Truth is different from belief and faith; both belief and faith can be misguided and are often wrong.

Belief is confidence that something is true. It may not be true, but you have confidence that it is, and you may even act upon it. Acting on belief is called faith. Faith, in most contexts, is a verb-not a noun. It is not something you are or something you have; it is what you are doing based upon your belief. However, faith alone does not mean the belief is truth. History is full of misguided beliefs and the faithful action they brought.

In World War II, Nazi Germany and Imperialist Japan believed they would conquer the world. Their populations held a belief that led to faith in their leaders. This faithful action took the world to war, but their actions proved untrue. It was only a belief, not the truth; the world did not fall to them. It was not their truth against our truth; it was a lie against the truth. Far too often we are taken in by strong belief, and our actions are often disastrous. Bad mistakes are often caused by misplaced beliefs. This is the success of con men: getting you to act on your belief in them.

If you do not know the truth when you find it, you will follow the one with the greatest story. That is what happens in politics, business and even religion--following the person who sounds the best. Picking leaders today is a display of charisma and developed skills of persuasion, not evidence of truth. Once you take a stand on substance and truth, the world will come after you.

Misery loves company, and finding the truth about racism and opportunity will make those in misery jealous and angry with you. They will call you names because that is all they have left. The only power liberals have is our fear of being called names. At the very hint of being called "hateful," "mean-spirited," "racist" or any other of their very colorful names, we back up and apologize. Let us stop backing up and stop apologizing.

I will leave you with advice my father gave me on handling name-calling. He said, " If you are engaged in an intellectual debate and reduce your opponent to name calling, you have won." Conservatives debate the issues on facts rather than emotions; liberals can only debate on emotions.

They are always talking about their "intentions"; we are interested only in the "results." Sometime it seems like we are from different planets, does it not? No matter what they have done in the past, the future action is based solely on intentions. It reminds me of a rapist telling his victim his "intentions" are to make love to her.

Therefore, when I began my journey from the liberal Berkeley militant student to a right-wing Christian conservative, I was immediately attacked. I was called everything but a child of God. My best friends and longtime acquaintances called me a long list of names. I was "Uncle Tom," "Sellout," "Europeanized," "Handkerchief head" and many others.

How did I respond? What was my reaction to this vicious attack upon my character and honor? Was there a response to the names and hatred? Yes, there was, I responded with "the truth, right between their lies." The truth!

Knowledge is a powerful shield; it will keep you from much danger. I knew who "Uncle Tom" was; I have read the book <u>*Uncle Tom's Cabin*</u> by Harriet Beecher Stowe. I knew that a sellout was a slave who sold out the plans of escape to the master for a scrap of meat. The Master starved the slaves until we became the only Black people on the planet who include pig guts, noses, ears, feet, tails and even the skin as part of our diet. The "sellout" would do anything for a scrap of meat, even disclose the plans of escape.

However, what would I disclose to "master" today? Would I go to the "White man" and tell him I have proof of your plans to educate yourself? Perhaps I will sell out the plans of leaving the plantation or providing better schools for the children. What danger could a "sellout" pose today? None! (Unless you are still on the plantation depending on "master" for any and everything.) If "master" is still in control and still responsible for your security, you should fear the "sellout." However, if you are free, the "sellout" can have no effect to you. I knew that the only way I could be a sellout to someone would be for that person to still be a slave.

A sellout could only sell out another slave, never a free person. Therefore, if you think I am a sellout, perhaps you should stop thinking like a slave. It is hard to think freely after living like a slave, but you must and you can.

When I said we are in control of the drugs and guns in our neighborhood, some whining cry-baby from the lewd left would say, "We don't have any airplanes and gun factories; the White man brings this into our neighborhoods." Such a thought is saying the White man has not only more power over your community, but it also says we have no control over our emotions. Even if the CIA brought drugs into the community, even if mad scientists created AIDS to exterminate Black people and even if the FBI allows guns into our community, so what? How much cocaine would I have to pour out on your lawn to get you to sell it to your own child? How many guns would I need to bring into your home to get you to murder your brother? Are we not at least in control of our personal actions? Is the White man so powerful he controls our voluntary actions?

AIDS is a disease that you have to go out and get. It is a pro-active disease; you must do something to get it. It does not come and get you through the air, water or food. There is some action taken on your part to acquire the disease. That is why it is called "Acquired" Immune Deficiency--you must get it; it does not get you. So control the activities associated with "acquiring" the disease, and we will not have to worry about the White man and his conspiracies.

We may have no control over drug smuggling from Columbia, or gun running. However, can we control our children and community? Where are the militants of the 1960's marching against the gang members instead of against the "White corporate structure?" Where is the call for "burn, baby, burn" in front of the crack house? Where are the strong Black men confronting the pimp, demanding he free those women caught in his trap? The whole community will march on the police station the minute some Black person is slightly misused by police. However, no one will shout disapproval when the system abuses your own child in school by giving out condoms, graduating illiterate children and teaching self-hate instead of self-motivation.

As a young man, I began the journey off of the plantation, and I found out that the hardest thing was to begin. Just to think of myself being on a plantation was insulting. I had to admit how wrong I was about myself and about my possibilities. I had to face the fact that I was misled by many people whom I respected. That is the only way a con man can succeed, by getting you to respect him. The journey was delayed by taking time trying to convince friends and associates they were going in the wrong direction.

To try to change others before they are willing to change themselves is a very frustrating and draining task. I had to stop arguing and debating with them because we were speaking two different languages, and I was getting nowhere. I was analyzing with logic, while they were reacting with emotions. I had to begin associating with people who would feed me knowledge and clarity.

The results were amazing to watch. You find yourself turning from those you thought were your friends towards those you thought were your enemies. It will not take long before you realize not just how wrong you had been, but why you were led to think that way. In order for master to keep control over the plantation, we must be full of fear and suspicion of others. The slaves used to say, "We gon get dim damn Yankees" and go off to fight against their own freedom. All of this "don't trust: the White man, Republicans, rich, capitalist, corporations" are the same as "dim damn Yankees." They are just a mirage to keep you out in the fields working to maintain your own slavery.

I did not change; I still had a passionate desire to help my community. America changed and I wanted to participate and not be passed over. It takes courage to fight for one's freedom; it takes more than courage to take the advantage of that freedom. Once I understood the real obstacles of Black Americans to control the gangs, drugs, teen pregnancies and other curses on our community, I began to speak out. My newspaper articles, public speeches, radio programs and television appearances all came from a desire to sound an alarm.

I could have stayed quiet and enjoyed my life and successful career. However, I was still a warrior and the battle was not over. I was still a messenger and the message had not been fully delivered. My message is clear: "It's OK To Leave The Plantation."

The beginning!!!

Raw Data
From the United States Census Bureau

Education
In 1995, 74 percent of African Americans aged 25 and over had at least a high school diploma and 13 percent held at least a Bachelor's degree, up from 51 percent and 8 percent, respectively, in 1980.

The proportion of African Americans aged 25 to 29 who had completed high school improved significantly from 1985 to 1995—from 81 percent to 87 percent. The share of young adult Whites in the same age group remained unchanged—at about 87 percent.

High school dropout rates for African American and White students in 1994 were around 5 percent.

Income and Poverty
Between 1994 and 1995, the median income of African American households rose 3.6 percent in real terms to $22,393, while the median income of White households increased 2.2 percent. The difference between these percentage changes was not statistically significant. The income of Asian and Pacific Islander households was unchanged; the small sample sizes for this population do not allow us to determine that there are any differences in their income changes from those of other racial or ethnic groups. The poverty rate for African Americans declined between 1994 and 1995, from 30.6 percent to 29.3 percent.

Population

On October 1, 1996, there were an estimated 33.7 million African Americans in the United States, comprising 12.7 percent of the total population. Their median age was 29.4 years.

It has projected that the African American population will grow more than twice as fast as the White population between 1995 and 2050. The African American population would increase 2 million by 2000, 7 million by 2010, and 17 million by 2030. By the middle of the next century, the African American population would nearly double its present size to 61 million.

In March 1994, 18.1 million or 55 percent of all African Americans lived in the South, 17 percent in the Northeast, 20 percent in the Midwest, and 8 percent in the West. The African American share of the total U.S. population is expected to increase from 12.6 percent in 1995 to 12.9 percent in 2000, 14 percent in 2020, and 15 percent in 2050.

After 2016, more African Americans than non-Hispanic Whites are expected to be added to the U.S. population each year.

Business

The number of African American-owned businesses increased from 424,165 in 1987 to 620,912 in 1992—growing 46 percent, or 20 percentage points more than U.S. businesses as a whole.

African American-owned business receipts increased from $19.8 billion in 1987 to $32.2 billion in 1992, an increase of 63 percent.

Receipts for African American-owned firms averaged $52,000 per firm, compared with $193,000 for all U.S. firms.

Fifty-six percent of African American-owned firms had receipts under $10,000. Less than 1 percent had receipts of $1 million or more.

The New York metro area had the most African American-owned firms, with 39,404, followed closely by Washington, D.C. (37,988) and Los Angeles (32,645).

Occupation and Earnings

In March 1994, the proportion of White males (27 percent) employed in managerial and professional jobs were nearly two times that of African American males (15 percent).

However, African American males were twice as likely as White males to work in service occupations (20 percent versus 10 percent).

Marital Status

In 1980, 45 percent of all African American women 15 years old and over were currently married; by 1995, the figure had declined to 38 percent. For African American men, the corresponding figures were 49 percent and 43 percent.

Children

In 1993, there were 10.7 million African American children under age 18. Thirty-six percent of those children lived with both parents; 54 percent with their mothers only. In comparison, 79 percent of non-Hispanic White children under age 18 lived in two-parent families and 16 percent lived with their mothers only.

In 1993, about four in 10 African American preschoolers were cared for by grandparents or other relatives besides their fathers while their mothers worked, compared to only about two in 10 White children. Care by grandparents was especially important to African American families, accounting for one-fifth of all arrangements used for preschoolers.

LIFT EVERY VOICE!

We owe so much to those who came before us. For their struggles and sacrifices we celebrate their victory. From the tears and misery they endured, we gain our strength.

To all who struggled and died, to all who resisted and suffered, to those who lived a life not worth living to preserve life for us...I dedicate our song.

The Negro National Anthem

Lift every voice and sing
Till earth and heaven ring,
Ring with the harmonies of Liberty;
Let our rejoicing rise
High as the listening skies,
Let it resound loud as the rolling sea.

Sing a song full of the faith that the dark past has taught us,
Sing a song full of the hope that the present has brought us,
Facing the rising sun of our new day begun
Let us march on till victory is won.

Stony the road we trod,
Bitter the chastening rod,
Felt in the days when hope unborn had died;
Yet with a steady beat,
Have not our weary feet
Come to the place for which our fathers sighed?

We have come over a way that with tears have been watered,
We have come, treading our path through the blood of the slaughtered,
Out from the gloomy past,
Till now we stand at last
Where the white gleam of our bright star is cast.

God of our weary years,
God of our silent tears,
Thou who has brought us thus far on the way;
Thou who has by Thy might
Led us into the light,
Keep us forever in the path, we pray.

Lest our feet stray from the places, Our God, where we met Thee;
Lest, our hearts drunk with the wine of the world, we forget Thee;

Shadowed beneath Thy hand,
May we forever stand.
True to our GOD,
True to our native land

LIFT EVERY VOICE AND SING (1900)
by James Weldon Johnson
Originally written by Johnson for a presentation in celebration of the birthday of Abraham Lincoln. This was originally performed in Jacksonville, Florida, by children.
The popular title for this work is: *The Negro National Anthem*

167

Certificate of Forgiveness

We have entered an era that is forcing us to reexamine our culture. The President of the United States, Bill Clinton, is discussing his memories of church burnings. These are memories of events that have never occurred. Our president is considering apologizing for slavery; however, I do not think he has any slaves. His apology is on behalf of a government that did not participate in the slave trade. We are under the Union government, not the Confederate government. His apology will be towards people who are not slaves today. The nation is now thinking of race relations because the President does not believe the Civil War is over.

We now have a race panel that cannot agree if black conservatives have a voice with black liberals. I will not mention the assumption that white liberals have a voice in the debate, but not white conservatives.

It is my opinion that all of the guilt white America is feeling has no real benefit. It will encourage acceptance of punishments for crimes and sins of ancestors. I believe that kind of guilt will cause more harm than good.

Therefore, if you are white and feel guilty over what your ancestors may have done to mine, allow me to forgive you. If you feel you should be punished for the crimes of the past, I offer you official forgiveness. If you accept this forgiveness, you must agree to enjoy life as a free productive citizen of America. Free and equal to participate on merit and in the spirit of competition, not reparation. If you agree, I hereby offer you my, *Certificate of Forgiveness*!

Certificate of Forgiveness!

Whereas, *we have found, in the course of history, that white Europeans took and held captive Black Africans, as slaves.*

Whereas, *for hundreds of years the white Europeans did on occasion, subject the aforementioned Black Africans, held as slaves, to the most inhumane treatment possible.*

Whereas, *we have found some of the descendants of the aforementioned white European slave holders are still feeling guilt (real or imagined) over the treatment of the aforementioned Black African slaves.*

Whereas, *we believe that continued guilt (real or imagined) is counterproductive to building forgiveness, trust and cooperation among all Americans, and furthermore believe distrust weakens our nation.*

Now Therefore I, *Clarence Mason Weaver,* president of *"The Committee to Restore America,"* *being found to be a descendent of the aforementioned Black African slaves, do hereby, by the authority of my ancestry, certify that all guilt, shame, and debt (real or imagined) of _____, found to be a descendent of white Europeans, is hereby forever forgiven and forgotten.*
Further_____*, is hereby released of all shame, guilt and debt of the white European slave holders (real or imagined) and may continue as a full citizen of the United States of America without the burden of apology, self-sacrifice or lowered self-esteem.*

Signed this_____day of _____in the year of our Lord, _____.

Clarence Mason Weaver_____, President

"The Committee to Restore America"
PO Box 1764 Oceanside, CA 92051

169

Endnotes

Chapter Three

1. Richard Hofstadter, *Great Issues in American History From the Revolution to the Civil War*, (New York: Vintage Books, 1958) pp.410-411.

2. Herbert Aptheker, *The American Negro Slave Revolts* (New York, 1943)

3. Information Please Almanac Atlas & Yearbook 1994 47th edition (Boston & New York: Houghton Mifflin Company) p. 412.

Chapter Five

4. Margaret Sanger, Manuscript Division Research Department, Library of Congress (Washington, 1977).

5. Jacqueline J. Cissel, Director of Social and Cultural studies for the Indian Family Institute in Indianapolis, Indiana, in a speech given before the National Minority Politics conference in Houston, Texas, Sept. 1994.

6. Hattie Carwell, *Blacks in Science - Astrophysicist to Zoologist (*Hicksville, New York: Exposition Press, 1977)pp. 75-96.

7. U.S. Department of Commerce, Economics and Statistics Administration Bureau of the Census, (Washington, D.C., Sept. 1993) pp. 1-9.

Chapter Seven

8. "GOP Making Inroads With Black Votes," *National Minority Politics,* January 1995, p. 33.

9. Lerone Bennett, Jr., *Before the Mayflower, A History of Black America* (Harmondsworth, Middlesex, England: Penguin Books-6th Edition) pp. 441-516.

10. Ibid.

Glossary

Abolition: A social movement that raised the moral question of whether men should own slaves. It was motivated by blacks, whites, freemen and slaves, but was primarily a Christian movement. Abolitionists' political strength came when they formed the Republican party in 1854 and nominated Abraham Lincoln for president in 1860.

Apartheid: A form of government and social system of white rule in South Africa. Apartheid was designed to ensure the continued rule of the white minority. Its concepts are similar to "Jim Crow" laws but reached much further than discrimination in eating and marriage. Apartheid controlled every aspect of life for black people in South Africa, including education, employment, place of residence and civil rights. Its overthrow was the focal point of the world's condemnation of South Africa.

Jim Crow: A system of laws and attitudes designed to segregate blacks and whites and keep them from eating together or marrying each other. They are best remembered for the "colored only" and "whites only" signs that appeared in the deep South. Jim Crow laws also influenced some "unwritten laws" and a lifestyle of "blacks knowing their place."

Oreo: This term means "black on the outside but white on the inside" and describes a black person "acting white" or trying to "be white." Commonly used to describe black people who speak proper English (white talk) or live outside the designated area for Blacks (plantation) or do not follow the multi-cultural directions of the so-called black leaders.

Overseer: A worker placed in charge of the plantation, field or house. The overseer answered to the master and enforced the law on the plantation.

Red Lining: A common practice more associated with Northern racism. Banks, Realtors and other service businesses would draw boundaries on city maps of areas in which they would secretly keep black customers from doing business. Drawn in red pen or pencil, this "red lining" made it difficult for black people to borrow money or rent in certain areas.

Sellout: This name was originally used to describe a slave who sold escape plans, usually for a small scrap of meat. This resulted in the deaths of slaves and was considered the lowest action of all. Today it is often used to describe black people who do not follow the black leaders or popular directions of society.

Slave Breaker: The slave who would carry out punishment for the master. Being very well trained with the whip, he would administer lashes "properly" without disabling the slave, allowing him or her to continue work. He was, in many cases, the executioner of the plantation.

Slave Driver: The highest position of a field slave. The "driver" forced the slaves to and from the fields like a sheepherder. He was the most feared and detested slave on the plantation. He kept order and issued punishment.

Uncle Tom: Originally a character in Harriet Beecher Stowe's _Uncle Tom's Cabin_ but soon became a name used to describe weak-minded slaves who would rather serve the master than fight for freedom. The character of the book was courageous and had strong Christian faith, but today the name is one of the greatest insults reserved for a black person.

Are you looking for a motivational speaker for your conference or meeting? Make your next gathering exciting, educational and unforgettable!

Clarence Mason Weaver brings the following experience and expertise including:

Radio Personality

Newspaper Columnist

Motivational Conference Speaker/Lecturer

Political Consultant

Business/Investment Expert

U.C. Berkeley Graduate: Political Science

Vietnam Veteran: U.S. Navy

Congressional Intern

Bilingual: English, Swahili

Clarence Mason Weaver would enjoy the opportunity to speak at your next meeting.

For more information, call 760-758-7448

or write to:

P.O. Box 1764

Oceanside, CA 92051

Would you like to order this book for a friend?
Fill out a form below and send it with a check to:
Mason Media Company
P.O. Box 1764, Oceanside, California 92051

Name_____
Address_____
City_____State_____
Zip_____Phone_____
Is this a gift?_____

Please send a check or money order for $20.00
to: P.O. Box 1764, Oceanside, CA 92051

Name_____
Address_____
City_____State_____
Zip_____Phone_____
Is this a gift?_____

Please send a check or money order for $20.00
to: P.O. Box 1764, Oceanside, CA 92051

Name_____
Address_____
City_____State_____
Zip_____Phone_____
Is this a gift?_____

Please send a check or money order for $20.00
to: Mason Media Company
P.O. Box 1764, Oceanside, CA 92051

Let us help you self-publish your book

We have had a number of experiences while self-publishing this book. There were many things we had to learn and many surprises along the way. We have discovered experts in editing, writing, graphic arts and many other fields that may be helpful to a self-publishing author. If you wish to contact us concerning publishing your book, let us know.

We ask that you not send manuscripts but give us an idea of what your project is. Self-publishing can be very exciting and rewarding. We would like to help you avoid possible mistakes along the way.

You can contact me at:
Mason Media Company
Mason Weaver, President
P.O. Box 1764, Oceanside, CA, 92051
Office and Fax 760-758-7448
e-mail: camason@ix.netcom.com

NOTES